"With a foot in both cultures and a sensitivity to the arguments of all sides, Carroll presents *Christians at the Border* to sort through the complicated and confusing immigration debate with nuance. He goes further than many studies by examining the question with a theological and biblical eye, a factor frequently ignored in what is often a shrill debate. Perspective is what such a complicated discussion requires, and that is what this book delivers. Read and learn."

— **Darrell Bock**, Dallas Theological Seminary

"Immigration issues grip American politics and opinions. But what does the Bible say? What is at the heart of the Christian view on immigration? Danny Carroll's voice on this issue is like no other. He is bilingual and bicultural; he is a Bible scholar and a committed Christian. Let him help shape your thinking and challenge your heart to be thoroughly Christian."

— **Leith Anderson**, National Association of Evangelicals

"Danny Carroll's goal of providing Christians with a biblical and theological framework to participate in the US immigration debate *as Christians* is met brilliantly in *Christians at the Border*. Even as he acknowledges that the Bible does not give us a specific policy blueprint, he demonstrates that Scripture provides important and clear principles that allow us to address the issue from a Christian perspective. *Christians at the Border* provides Christians of various political perspectives a framework from which to begin a conversation together about how to address the issue of immigration in the United States."

— **Juan Francisco Martínez**, Fuller Theological Seminary

"Carroll's grasp of the problems presented by immigration—political, economic, and familial—is balanced, restrained, and profound. On one level the book is a thorough presentation of the 'secular' facts, and on a deeper level those facts and problems are brought into contact with biblical and theological insight. Evangelicals will be well informed on both levels. Catholic leaders, too, with their steadily developed approach to the same problem, will find in Carroll a complementary and supporting vision. The need for a specifically Christian approach, a vision of the welcoming of the stranger, is evident, and Carroll supplies that need admirably. Protestants and Catholics of all political leanings need to pay attention to this book."

— **William M. Shea**, College of the Holy Cross

"Danny Carroll R. has the kind of scholarly background in biblical studies and cultural anthropology that the subject calls for. He articulates well the facts, questions, and perspectives. He proposes answers, or at least gives suggestions, that are both compassionate and realistic, and he does so from a soundly biblical and distinctly Christian point of view. But this is not just a well-researched book. The author has both personal history and experience that make him the right person to approach the current immigration issues in a penetrating and sympathetic way. This man and his book deserve serious consideration in the current debate."

—**Richard E. Averbeck**, Trinity Evangelical Divinity School

"A timely, must-read book for the church in the United States. The thinking of many American citizens concerning Hispanic immigration is being shaped by heated and emotional political debate both locally and nationally. M. Daniel Carroll R.'s book helps us think through this complex issue clearly and soberly by presenting a well-documented historical and biblical perspective on immigration and people movements. This book will help the American church see God's heart on this matter and act sensibly, compassionately, and biblically toward the stranger or alien living and working among us."

—**Dennis J. Rivera**, Central Latin American District Council of the Assemblies of God, Denver, Colorado

"Carroll provides a good summary of the different positions regarding immigration in the United States and helps readers discover God's heart for immigrants. *Christians at the Border* is a valuable resource in thinking about immigration from a Christian perspective. I highly recommend it."

—**Octavio J. Esqueda**, Southwestern Baptist Theological Seminary

"Combining prophetic zeal with a tender, pastoral tone, Carroll calls on Christians to adopt a distinctively Christian disposition to the issue of undocumented immigrants and even more importantly to the *people* who find themselves in this situation. He argues convincingly that for Christians, the ethic of compassion and commitment to the well-being of the marginalized must take precedence over legality. If we heed his plea, immigrants will know when they encounter us that they have crossed the border into a land of distinctively gracious people."

—**Daniel I. Block**, Wheaton College

"In this biblical primer on immigration, Danny Carroll does not make policy recommendations but does provide attitude checks for believers as we enter the great immigration debate taking place in our country. With the skill of a biblical scholar, the heart of a prophet, and the rich background of a Guatemalan-American, Dr. Carroll speaks Solomonesque wisdom that will help us all."

—**Don Sweeting**, Cherry Creek Presbyterian Church, Greenwood Village, Colorado

CHRISTIANS
at the BORDER

Immigration, the Church,
and the Bible

M. Daniel Carroll R.

Foreword by Samuel Rodríguez
Afterword by Ronald J. Sider

B
Baker Academic
a division of Baker Publishing Group
Grand Rapids, Michigan

Published by Baker Academic
a division of Baker Publishing Group
P.O. Box 6287, Grand Rapids, MI 49516-6287
www.bakeracademic.com

Printed in the United States of America

Library of Congress Cataloging-in-Publication Data
Carroll R., M. Daniel.
    Christians at the border : immigration, the church, and the Bible / M. Daniel Carroll R.
        p.   cm.
    Includes bibliographical references and index.
    ISBN 978-0-8010-3566-1 (pbk.)
    1. Emigration and immigration in the Bible. 2. Emigration and immigration—Religious aspects—Christianity. I. Title.
BS680.E38C37 2008
261.8'36—dc22   2007048177

Al pueblo hispano—
peregrinos en tierra ajena,
artesanos de una vida nueva,
semilla de esperanza—
paz y ánimo para el largo camino

To the Christian church in the United States:
may we never forget that we are
sojourners in a strange land,
and that among us
there is neither Jew nor Greek

CONTENTS

Foreword by Samuel Rodríguez   9
Acknowledgments   13
Introduction   15

1. Hispanic Immigration:
   Invasion or Opportunity?   25
2. Of Immigrants, Refugees, and Exiles:
   Guidance from the Old Testament, Part I   63
3. The Law and the Sojourner:
   Guidance from the Old Testament, Part II   91
4. Welcoming the Stranger:
   Guidance from the New Testament   113
5. Where Do We Go from Here?
   Final Thoughts   135

Afterword by Ronald J. Sider   141
Appendix: Selected Resources   144
Notes   154
Index   173

FOREWORD

Samuel Rodríguez
National Hispanic Christian
Leadership Conference

Embedded in the narrative of the American experience is the thread of a culture committed to righteousness and justice. In *Christians at the Border*, M. Daniel Carroll R. calls on those foundational elements of our society in order to address the issue of immigration from a biblical, historical, economic, and kingdom perspective, and he succeeds in contextualizing the immigration issue and transforming the platform from a debate to a dialogue among Americans, and certainly among fellow Christians.

As I found myself traveling from California to Washington DC weekly for a year and a half, attempting to broker a viable compromise on this issue, three fundamental questions arose. First, how should Christians respond to the immigration issue? Second, what do Americans, and especially American Christians, need to know in order to respond in a manner consistent with our Judeo-Christian value system? And finally—the question raised by reporters, members of congress, senators, and White House staffers alike—does the Bible provide any guidance on the issue of immigration? *Christians at the Border* offers answers to these questions. This book will help the majority culture and Hispanics begin to think about and respond to this issue primarily as Christians and citizens of God's kingdom. Without a doubt, Carroll offers the theological and biblical framework in which the followers of Jesus Christ can analyze, evaluate, and act in respect to immigration, and the Hispanic immigrant community in particular, in a manner that complements the ethos of our Christian journey.

It is impossible to have a thorough understanding of the current immigration discussion without taking into consideration the dynamics of the three-legged stool on which the future of immigration in America rests: cultural identity, economic impact, and Hispanic Christianity. Carroll begins the journey of framing the biblical approach toward immigration by describing the socio-ethno convergence of these three driving forces in an unbiased, objective, and sound manner. As a result, Christians committed to a transformational missiology will be better equipped to address the immigration-related issues of cultural identity, assimilation, and economic impact, as well as the global ramifications, with sound biblical support. Certainly, the most intriguing fact stemming from the data presented by Professor Carroll addresses the opportunities that exist for both America and, more importantly, God's kingdom. I wholeheartedly believe that by the time readers finish *Christians at the Border*, their approach will change from debating the immigration issue to discussing the immigration opportunity.

Danny takes us on a journey from Genesis to the New Testament in order to extrapolate biblical principles and truths pertaining to the immigrant community. In a persuasive, logical, and systematic fashion, *Christians at the Border* enables the reader to view the immigrant as a sojourner. Furthermore, this book examines the historical role of America's faith communities, offering a foundation for them to act in the spirit of reconciliation by exposing the nexus of both compassion and the rule of law within an enriching canopy for our nation and for the kingdom of God.

Finally, we cannot deny the fact that the immigration issue has the potential of either polarizing our society or enriching our narrative. My hope is for the latter. A hope that the spirit of compassion, love, and tolerance stemming from the Judeo-Christian ethos and embedded in our collective narrative will once again prevail and embrace righteousness and justice for all. A hope that the Christian community will rise up, speak vociferously from the pulpit of reconciliation to all corridors of our society, and demand an end to extreme ideologies from all sides of this debate.

We must recognize that at the various crossroads of American history, when despair and desperation coalesced around the inevitable defeat of reason, oracles of truth arose to articulate and disseminate to the masses the moral imperative of sound, practical, and graceful deliberation. From the revolutionary war to the abolitionist movement to the struggle for civil rights in the 1960s, writers, scholars, and clergy have presented the case for truth and righteousness in a way that is compatible with the values of a biblical worldview. In *Christians at the Border*, Professor Carroll continues in this very prophetic and practical role. Undoubtedly, even when—it is no longer a matter of if—legislation is passed that deals with the various dynamics of the immigration debate, the content of this book will serve as a primer for immigration issues for years to come.

ACKNOWLEDGMENTS

I would like to thank several individuals for helping make this book a reality. Jim Kinney of Baker Academic first listened to my ideas for this book with his usual patience and graciousness. Then he worked hard to make the project a reality. I am grateful that he took on its vision of offering to the "ordinary Christian" a more informed reflection on the Hispanic presence within the United States. Jonathan Jameson, a former student of mine at Denver Seminary, spent many hours tracking down materials on the Internet and saved me precious time by compiling the index. Giles Clasen, another student, surprised me one day when work on the book was already under way by informing me that he was a photojournalist. He is the one who took the pictures that so richly enhance the front and back covers.

Two Hispanic pastors in the Denver area have been wonderful encouragers. Erik Valenzuela, a Guatemalan, and Jorge Barbarán, a Peruvian, were keys to the successful launching of IDEAL (Instituto para el Desarrollo y Adiestramiento de Líderes), our Spanish-speaking program at Denver Seminary. They have been models of ministerial dedication and joy, and I am glad to call them friends. Federico Maes, a lawyer of Spanish-American descent and an ardent student of the Bible, has amazed me with his boundless energy and deep commitment to his people and the Hispanic church. He, too, is a friend and model, whom the Lord in his grace has allowed to cross my path. I have learned much also from the ministers of the Alianza Ministerial Hispana, who sometimes were not quite sure what to do with a seminary professor.

Denver Seminary, in particular its president Dr. Craig Williford, is visionary in moving into the uncharted waters of Hispanic cultural and church life. Not many seminaries possess either the courage or the commitment to serve all for the sake of the kingdom of God. It has been a joy to start IDEAL and to turn the leadership of Hispanic initiatives over to Wilmer Ramírez, a Honduran and former student of mine from SETECA (Seminario Teológico Centroamericano), the seminary in Guatemala City where I taught for many years before coming to Denver. The journey into this new world is just beginning, even if no one is sure how things will unfold along the way!

Finally, I am grateful to my family. To my mother, Edit Rodas Carroll, for reminding me of the importance of *nuestra guatemalidad*. I am blessed with a wonderful wife, Joan, who has lived with this complex character of mixed heritage for over thirty years. Countless times she has listened patiently to this *Quijote*, who always seems to be on the quest to understand himself and life as a cultural hybrid, and she has been willing to venture continuously across cultural boundaries with me. I only hope that I have been a worthy guide. Our sons, Matthew and Adam, have been raised in the two very different worlds of the United States and Guatemala. My prayer is that they continue to learn to admire this country, but never lose *el amor por la patria de su juventud*; that they learn the language of efficiency and technology, but nurture in their souls *el idioma del amor y de los sueños*; and that in their hearts they always find a place for both the eagle and *el quetzal*.*

August 2007

*The *quetzal* is the national bird of Guatemala.

INTRODUCTION

I am the son of a Guatemalan mother and an American
father. My parents met in New Orleans after the Second
World War, were married in Guatemala, and then moved
to the United States. I was born and grew up in Houston,
but my life was different in many ways from most.

My mother made a point of raising my brother and
me bilingual and bicultural. Speaking both English and
Spanish was something natural. We frequently had family
and friends from Guatemala come through our home, and
my parents had several Cuban friends in the area whom
we would visit; in time my brother would marry a Cuban
woman. As boys, my brother and I spent entire summers
in Guatemala. We would stay with family after our parents
returned to the US, and during those times we grew to know
the country and participated in Latin American culture in
many ways. During several summers our parents enrolled
us in a school called La Preparatoria (the Guatemalan academic year runs from mid-January to mid-October). The
school was located across the street from the central post
office in downtown Guatemala City and was not far from
the coffee shop our grandmother owned, across the street

from the national palace. At noon, when classes would break for a couple of hours (a Latin American tradition that has almost completely disappeared because of the size of cities today), we would walk from school to Le Petit Café and then go on to our grandmother's house for lunch before heading back to classes in the afternoon.

A decade later things changed drastically from those more halcyon days. There was a massive earthquake in 1976. The school we had attended was one of the buildings destroyed, and my grandmother's neighborhood was forever changed. I, too, was now a different person. I had finished college, where I had come to a personal faith in Christ. I was also recently married and a first-year seminary student. But even harsher times lay ahead for Guatemala.

After seminary my wife and I moved to Guatemala in the summer of 1982. This was during the troubled presidency of Efraín Ríos Montt. Since the early 1960s, Guatemala had been in an armed conflict, but the war escalated over time to horrific proportions and was at its most violent just before our arrival. The rest of the isthmus was also in turmoil. The hostilities in El Salvador were at their peak; the Sandinistas were in power in Nicaragua, and the Contra were seeking to oust them. A peace treaty between the Guatemalan government and the guerrilla forces would eventually be signed in December 1996, but by then the fighting had taken untold thousands of lives and left many more widowed, orphaned, and displaced.[1]

During that fascinating yet tragic time, we raised our family in the capital city, where I taught at El Seminario Teológico Centroamericano (SETECA). After fifteen years there, we returned to the United States, and I assumed a position at Denver Seminary. I continue, however, as an adjunct at SETECA, so I am able to be in our beloved Guatemala every year to teach and spend time with friends and family in that world so profoundly rooted in my soul.

16

The war changed Guatemala in many ways, some of which are inseparably connected to the topic of this book. Many left the country—some fleeing political persecution, others merely looking for a new start, one with the promise of a better and more peaceful life. The United States was the natural destination for most. In the decade since the end of that conflict, international economic realities have attracted even more Guatemalans to the US. Of course, millions from Mexico and other Latin American countries have made their way north, too.

A Unique Perspective?

North America is changing and will never be the same. Spanish-speaking television networks (Univisión, Telemundo) are growing in influence; Latin American cuisine is becoming standard fare in many parts; music on the radio (and all sorts of handheld devices) is rocking to different beats, and the Latin Grammy Awards is an annual event; Jennifer López, Salma Hayek, Antonio Banderas, and other actors cross over between English- and Spanish-speaking roles; Latin Americans (players, managers, and now owners) dominate baseball, and soccer (*fútbol*) is gaining in popularity; Spanish newspapers and magazines are springing up everywhere; the Hispanic Chamber of Commerce, locally and nationally, wields growing clout; political parties are courting Hispanic voters and both houses of Congress have Hispanic members; the premier sports network ESPN also has ESPN–Deportes; any number of universities have Chicano or Latino/a departments and immigration research centers; many neighborhoods and shopping areas are taking on a new look; Cinco de Mayo celebrations are growing; the color of the work force is changing—the list could go on. "The 25 Most Influential Hispanics in America" was the cover story of the August 22, 2005, issue of *Time*, and countless other national magazines and local newspapers have carried reports and editorials on Hispanic immigration during the last few years.

What many fail to realize, however, is that most people of Hispanic descent are not newly arrived immigrants. Millions have been here for generations, and a multitude like myself are of mixed heritage. It is the *recent* surge in the numbers of Hispanics resulting from immigration that has generated unease.

> Too often discussions default to the passionate ideological arguments, economic wrangling, or racial sentiments that dominate national discourse.

I watch this seismic shift with great interest. My personal background and experience give me something of a distinctive point of view with respect to the complicated situation that is the immigration of Hispanics—more particularly, of undocumented Hispanics—into the United States. I grew up in this country, but always with a foot south of the border. A sizeable part of my professional life has been exercised in Guatemala (along with travel to many other Central and South American countries), and my research and writing often grow out of my passion for things Latin American and Hispanic. I feel equally comfortable in both English and Spanish, whether speaking, reading, or writing, and my heart and palate swing easily between both worlds. I teach a full load in English at Denver Seminary, but I also played a part in establishing a Spanish-speaking training program there (IDEAL: Instituto para el Desarrollo y Adiestramiento de Líderes). My wife and I are members of an Anglo church but also attend Hispanic churches, and for the last several years I have served on the board of the Alianza Ministerial Hispana (Hispanic Ministers Alliance) of metro-Denver.

In many ways, then, I stand between the majority culture and the Hispanic culture. I care for both, although I must admit my deepest longings are for my Guatemalan roots. My desire, though, is that what follows may speak in constructive ways to both sides of the divide. I do not stand in a neutral place, but I will strive to offer a fresh look at the national debate.

The Purpose of This Book

I am an Old Testament scholar by training, and I am also committed to the mission of the Christian church. In other words, I am concerned about how the Bible can orient the way the broader Christian community, denominations, local churches, and individual Christians understand their identity and role in the world today. The immigration of undocumented Hispanics is one area that all must respond to, and, of course, millions of these immigrants make some claim to Christian faith.

The topic is huge and extraordinarily complicated. I do not pretend to offer solutions to the myriad of contested issues or to propose some sort of legislative cure-all for the many problems. This book tries to do justice to the complexity of the current state of affairs. An appreciation of how complicated the situation is can help move us beyond the entrenched posturing and simplistic positions that often dominate the media and current politics. It should spur us all to seek a deeper wisdom, and herein lies the purpose of this book.

My intention is to try to move Christians to reconsider their starting point in the immigration debate. Too often discussions default to the passionate ideological arguments, economic wrangling, or racial sentiments that dominate national discourse. Among Christians, my experience has been that there is little awareness of what might be a divine viewpoint on immigration. This book is a modest attempt to help remedy that shortcoming. It is neither exhaustive nor comprehensive. Rather, it is designed as a primer for a more biblically and theologically informed approach to the topic.

The first chapter briefly surveys the history of Hispanic migration to the United States. It then articulates two of the main points of contention concerning undocumented immigrants—the potential impact on national identity and economics—but it also adds other relevant observations to each point that usually do not receive the attention they deserve. The chapter closes with another side of Hispanic life that at times is ignored but that should be fundamental to a Christian approach: the role of religion. Hispanic Christian churches, both Protestant and Catholic, are growing and vibrant. They are part of a worldwide trend of migrations that holds profound implications for the future of the Christian faith.

This turn to faith serves as a transition to the next three chapters, which are the heart of the book. Two chapters expound the material in the Old Testament that is pertinent to immigration. The third chapter attends to the New Testament's contribution. The biblical material has important things to say to Christians of both the majority and Hispanic cultures. All people from the Christian heritage can gather around this sacred Word, which they share, and listen to the voice of God. Christians must think about and act on Hispanic immigration *as Christians*.

This book is not an academic tome full of specialist jargon and bewildering charts. After each discussion of what the Bible has to offer to the topic, there is a section titled "Implications for Today." These sections are designed to stimulate thinking about how to apply the teachings of the relevant biblical material to the challenges of immigration. The endnotes direct the reader to additional data regarding social, economic, and political issues and biblical research. They are not at the level of a technical monograph, but they can be a helpful beginning for those who desire more information. The appendix is designed to be a resource tool.

It contains several selected bibliographies and lists a number of relevant Web sites. The indexes can help the reader quickly find topics, names, and biblical references used in the body of the book and in the endnotes. All in all, my hope is that *Christians at the Border* will be both informative and useful.

Defining Terms

What makes this discussion a bit more thorny is that the label *Hispanic* itself is contested by many. The word originally comes from *Hispania*, an ancient name for the Iberian Peninsula. In more formal Spanish, *Hispano* can still refer to things related to Spain. For example, Latin America (Mexico, Central and South America) is also called *Hispanoamérica*. In the United States, however, the term Hispanic came into common parlance as a category designation used by the Census Bureau for all people who are of Spanish or Latin American descent. This very broad category lumped together those from different countries, races, national histories, and even languages.[2] For this reason, not a few academics and activists eschew the term altogether as imprecise and an unjust imposition. They prefer the term *Latino* (feminine *Latina*). I certainly sympathize with this concern, but nonetheless I have decided to use Hispanic. This is the word most people are familiar with and the one regularly used in the media. My choice, therefore, is one of convenience and strategy: most readers of this book will be more familiar with the label Hispanic than with Latino.[3]

It also is helpful to distinguish between the terms *refugee* and *immigrant*. Refugees are those persons who have fled their country of origin out of fear of persecution because of their race, religion, social standing, or political views, or those who have escaped an armed conflict.[4] As these people seek another country where they can settle, they can also be called asylum seekers. Due to the violence in Central and South America from the 1970s to the 1990s large numbers sought asylum or refugee status in the United States, Canada, Europe, and elsewhere. Today, the major source of refugees looking for a new home is Africa. Thousands upon thousands are running away from hostilities in countries such as the Sudan, Somalia, and Zimbabwe. Many are housed in large camps, where they can be confined for years as they wait for sanctuary. The United Nations coordinates their placement with potential host countries through its High Commission for Refugees.

Immigrants, in contrast, are those who have moved to another country of their own volition and are usually seeking lengthy or permanent residence. Immigrants can enter either legally—through official ports of entry and according to the rules of the admissions policies established by the host country—or not. Those who have come into the United States by other means are frequently called illegal aliens.

I prefer the word *undocumented* rather than *illegal* for several reasons. Illegal can carry a pejorative connotation, suggesting by definition that the person is guilty of some act, has few scruples, and is prone to civil disobedience. This is not the case with the overwhelming majority of Hispanic immigrants. Most would gladly regularize their status with the government, but the present system simply does not provide appropriate avenues to do so. What these people lack is the proper documentation required by Washington and the workplace. They are not criminals. At the same time, the label *alien* can evoke the sense of someone unchangeably foreign and other, without hope of reconciliation or mediation. *Illegal aliens*, therefore, is unhelpfully prejudicial. *Undocumented immigrants* is a more just label and better represents the present reality. These people and the national response to their entry and presence are the focus of this book.

An Exhortation to the Reader

The title *Christians at the Border* is a double entendre. In a very real sense everyone in the United States has to take a political position about what is going on at the physical boundary with Mexico. Consciously or unconsciously, we all take a stand at that literal border, a stand that reflects our social, economic, and racial attitudes and situation. But for Christians there is an additional border. It is a metaphorical decision point. We must determine whether the place we choose to stand in the national debate will be based on the Word of God or whether we will ignore its teaching and defend our opinion on other grounds. This border, in other words, confronts us as a crossroads of faith and conviction.

Qué el Señor nos ilumine y otorgue entendimiento.
May the Lord illumine us and grant us understanding.

1

HISPANIC IMMIGRATION

Invasion or Opportunity?

On a steamy night in May 2003, over seventy men, women, and children crammed into a semi-trailer in Harlingen, Texas. They were on their way to a new life, and many looked forward to reuniting with loved ones who had preceded them to the United States. But soon that semi-trailer became a suffocating inferno. Nineteen died from heat exhaustion and suffocation in what some call "the worst immigrant tragedy in American history."[1]

Detectives John Bishop and Donald Young were working off duty as security at a baptismal party in a Hispanic neighborhood in Denver on May 8, 2005. Suddenly, what should have been a joyous celebration turned grisly. Raúl Gómez García shot both officers in the back, wounding Bishop and killing Young. Gómez García quickly fled the scene and made his way to Mexico. With the cooperation of law enforcement officials there, the suspect was arrested one month later. Colorado authorities sought to bring Gómez García to Denver for trial, but Mexican law prohibits extradition if there is the possibility of a sentence of life without parole or the death penalty. Eventually a compromise was reached, and Gómez García was sent to the United States that December. In late 2006 he was convicted and sentenced to eighty years in prison.

On December 12, 2006, US Immigration and Customs Enforcement officials raided Swift meat packing plants in Colorado, Texas, Iowa, Nebraska, Utah, Kentucky, and Minnesota. Their targets were immigrants who had used false documents to obtain employment. Hundreds were taken into custody, and several were summarily deported. Some decried the lack of due process and the thoughtless separation of parents from their children; others believed it was about time the government began to enforce the law.

José Antonio Gutiérrez, a Guatemalan orphaned as a child, made his way north several years ago to Los Angeles. He joined the Marines to help pay for his future university studies and as an expression of thanks to the US for giving him a chance for a different life. He was killed in Iraq on March 21, 2003, as one of the first casualties of the war. Gutiérrez was granted citizenship posthumously.[2]

Complicated landscape. Debate over Hispanic immigration can sometimes be a heated exchange of stories, a trading of emotive accounts of untimely deaths and unjust suffering. These stories are all too real, and therein lies their power to generate both compassion and anger. The terrible immigrant tale from Texas is one of many now in print that detail the travails of those who have braved the deserts of the Southwest, the wiles of the *coyotes*, and the watchful eyes of the border patrols. During the past decade, several thousand perished in an effort to cross the border.[3] These experiences have been celebrated in song, such as the hit "El Mojado" ("The Wetback") by the Guatemalan singer Ricardo Arjona, the song "En mi Bolivia" by the Bolivian Yuri Ortuño and La Nueva Proyección, and countless ballads sung by *Norteña* bands. The accounts are as varied as anything one can imagine. That has been my own perception as I have listened to immigrants open their hearts and tell of their trek northward. But citizens of this country have also suffered violence in car wrecks, robberies, and other crimes at the hands of undocumented immigrants, some of whom have been able to evade apprehension or conviction. These victims cry out for justice, too.[4]

These sensitive stories are symptoms of a larger set of challenges related to Hispanic immigration. The multiple issues seem intractable, the number of people overwhelming. Emotions run high, and rhetoric flourishes. Metaphors used in the media heighten the perception of a massive and uncontrollable influx of foreigners. Hispanic immigration is labeled a "flood," a "rising tide" or "tidal wave," a "horde," or an "invasion." Red flag language, such as "amnesty," the "war on terror," or the "terrible human cost," punctuates discussions that can degenerate into unfruitful diatribes. Innumerable publications, from the popular to the scholarly, and a growing number of Internet sites argue their particular points of view.

In response to these differing perceptions and needs of all kinds, activist organizations—from human rights groups to border vigilantes—have sprung into action to mobilize their audiences. Selective poll data bolster a spectrum of stances, even while more circumspect polls demonstrate variations within the general population regarding such pressing issues as the possibility of providing avenues to legal work status, residency, or citizenship.[5] In the midst of all this, many Hispanics have refused to remain passive onlookers. The nation has witnessed a few mass marches in several cities, but there are also more-formal, long-standing groups that are active in lobbying local, state, and national government, working in Hispanic neighborhoods, and networking immigrant organizations.

Both political parties recognize that the Hispanic population presents the potential for millions of votes. Recent elections witnessed increased efforts by Democrats and Republicans to woo these voters and convince them that their party's commitments reflect Hispanic concerns. Recent studies show that Hispanics do not vote in block and that they differ from their majority culture counterparts.[6] In the presidential elections of 2004 the Hispanic votes in California and Florida were as strikingly different as the voter profiles of each state (California is overwhelmingly Mexican and Central American; Florida is largely Cuban and Puerto Rican). Labor unions are also rallying to the immigrant cause, as they see the promise of new members to replace declining numbers. For their part, some undocumented workers visualize the unions as a means to secure better wages and protection in the workplace.

Structure of the chapter. In such a heated and convoluted atmosphere, is there any chance for thoughtful reflection? Was it always so complicated? How did we get to this point? A helpful place to begin is to take a succinct look at the history of Hispanic immigration to the United States. After this survey, I review two sets of issues that have been lightning rods: the possible effects of immigration on national identity and its impact on the economy. I add a component to each of these points that provides readers with a broader perspective on the realities "on the ground" and that is rarely considered in discussions on immigration. Events and issues are often more complicated than they may seem. Perhaps the truth on these matters lies in a more nuanced middle ground, between the opposite poles of closing the border with stiff enforcement and opening it indiscriminately to all who desire to come.

I consciously avoid throwing statistics at the reader. Statistics can be impressive, but they are always disputed and can be confusing. Those who want that information will find appropriate resources in the endnotes. My focus is on how the immigration of undocumented Hispanics is described and debated in the public sector. It is ideas and feelings that I am after, not numbers.

Yet another important dimension must be addressed by those who claim to be Christians, and with this the chapter will close: How are the newly arrived Hispanics affecting the landscape of the Christian faith in the United States? How might the presence of millions of Hispanic Christians—both Catholic and Protestant—inform one's position vis-à-vis immigration? Should arguments be limited to the cultural and the economic? This chapter closes by trying to refocus the discussion on Hispanic immigration with matters of faith and ministry.

A Brief History of Hispanic Immigration

A General Orientation

Primary factors. Several theories attempt to explain the causes and process of international migration.[7] Sorting through these various perspectives lies beyond the purview of this book, but some general observations can be made with respect to the United States. Immigration is neither a new phenomenon nor a recent political concern. It has been a topic of national interest since the colonial

> Immigration is neither a new phenomenon nor a recent political concern.

era. The internal issues, however, always have had a global backdrop.[8] That is, each major period of immigration to the United States has been part of larger migrations happening simultaneously around the world and, therefore, has been inseparable from the political, social, and economic conditions of other nations.

From the dawn of the republic, authorities have deliberated about who would be welcomed and who would be excluded. Originally, immigration was handled by the states, but the increased complications of monitoring the entrance of foreign peoples led the Supreme Court in 1875 to declare immigration to be the responsibility of the federal government. The Immigration Act of 1891 established the Office of the Superintendent of Immigration within the Treasury Department. Eventually this would develop into the Immigration and Naturalization Service (INS) and be moved to the Department of Justice. Recently, the INS was transferred to the jurisdiction of the Department of Homeland Security.

History demonstrates a recurring tension principally between economic concerns and different expressions of nativism. Nativism consists of feelings of fear of or hatred toward a foreign minority that is believed to threaten what is assumed to be the national culture. This is not to say that the twin poles of economics and nativism define the only public responses to immigration. The outlook of the American populace as a whole usually lies somewhere between the two. The United States has frequently been characterized by graciousness to outsiders, and it has absorbed millions of immigrants, refugees, and asylum seekers since its founding.

The economic factors that have motivated immigration to the United States have entailed the continuous interplay between a lack of opportunities in the country of origin (the push factor) and the drive to meet the needs of American business, industry, and farming (the pull factor). The contrary emotions of nativism have been generated by several dynamics, depending on the particular period and circumstances: religious sentiments, ignorance or rejection of unfamiliar customs, racism, educational levels, and competition for jobs. During the past 150 years the multiple conflicts between economic demands at home and abroad, popular opposition, the attitudes of organized labor, foreign policy, and the agendas of political parties have yielded a legacy of contradictory regulations and inconsistent enforcement. Confusing compromises and legal irregularities have reigned as politicians have sought to satisfy opposing constituencies.

Negative examples. Some early cases of immigrant restriction stand out. One of the most notorious was the treatment of Chinese immigrants for about a century. Beginning in the late 1840s, the needs in California in agriculture, mining, and the building of the railroads fueled a search for inexpensive manpower.[9] The solution was found in contracting workers from mainland China. Soon recruiting firms were established in Asia, and these collaborated with shipping firms to facilitate the movement of laborers to this country. The US government and Chinese authorities negotiated several trade agreements to legalize and regulate this traffic. As early as 1852, however, locals sought to block the importation of "coolies." Brutal racial discrimination persisted for decades. "Suspicious" Chinese females were not permitted entry in order to avoid births of those of Chinese origin on US soil (and so the right to citizenship, according to the Fourteenth Amendment); there were all kinds of restrictions placed on these immigrants at local levels, and violence exploded against them and their property on a number of occasions. This antipathy culminated in the Chinese Exclusion Act of 1882, which barred the introduction of any further Chinese labor and denied the Chinese any claim to citizenship; this prohibition was renewed on several occasions. Chinese were not accorded the right to become citizens until 1943 with the passage of the Chinese Exclusion Repeal Act (the Magnuson Act).

Another negative reaction to a large scale immigration occurred in the final quarter of the nineteenth century and the early years of the twentieth with the arrival of millions of Irish and southern Europeans, especially Italians.

31

Opposition arose from many quarters, based on the claim that these new groups were educationally and culturally inferior, a drain on the economy, and politically problematic. Moreover, in contrast to the general Protestant flavor of the majority culture of the day, these immigrants were overwhelmingly Catholic. All of these negative features, it was felt, would damage the American ethos. A quota system to limit the admission of immigrants from certain countries was put into place with the immigration Acts of 1921 (the Quota Act) and 1924 (the Johnson-Reed Act).

The cruelest chapter in the history of immigration to the US, and the one with the most tragic consequences, of course, was the forced relocation here of millions of Africans that occurred between the seventeenth and the early nineteenth centuries. The opportunity for integration into national life would not become a possibility until the Emancipation Proclamation of 1863, and it would not become a constitutional right until the ratification of the Thirteenth Amendment in 1865 and of the Fourteenth Amendment in 1868. Nevertheless, true legal, cultural, educational, and sporting assimilation would have to await the efforts of the civil rights movement a century later. But even today, vestiges of prejudice and exclusion still remain.

Hispanic Immigration

1848–1940. Migration from Mexico and Latin America did not begin technically until 1848.[10] That was the year that the Treaty of Guadalupe-Hidalgo, which ended the Mexican-American War, was signed. With this agreement, Mexico ceded to the United States the territory that today makes up the states of California, Nevada, and Utah and parts of Arizona, New Mexico, Colorado, and Wyoming.[11] That this large swath of territory originally was part of Mexico means there has been a Hispanic presence in the United States for over a century and a half. The creation of the new national boundaries officially establishes the starting point for any immigration activity. For a number of years the land along the border of the two countries was not very populated. Several events changed that pattern between 1890 and 1929.

The prohibition against bringing in Chinese workers played a role in triggering the arrival of Mexican workers. Agriculture and industry had to look elsewhere to replace the loss of Chinese labor, and substitutes were readily at hand to the south. Ironically, the exclusion of one immigrant people opened the door to another. Another key event was the outbreak of the First World War. Hundreds of thousands of Americans joined the armed services, and the war effort created the need for even more manpower in industry. That conflict, though, halted immigration from Europe. Once again Mexican workers were available to fill the gap. To this constellation of factors can be added the political and economic situation in Mexico at that time. The agricultural and industrial decisions of President Porfirio Díaz (1876–1910) created a large landless population desperate for work, ready to move to the United States where there was a continuing demand for labor. The Mexican Revolution (1910–17) drove many more across the border in search of safety.

The majority of those who came during this time span did not plan to set down permanent roots here. The goal for most was to acquire enough capital to be able to fund a new life back home. Many, of course, did stay. The US Border Patrol was founded in 1924. Though the immigration Acts of 1921 and 1924 established country-of-origin quotas and the Border Patrol had a presence, not much was done to stem the flow of workers from Mexico.

The situation dramatically changed toward the end of the 1920s. With the Stock Market crash of 1929, the onset of the Great Depression, and the desperate state of the job market, there was a backlash against foreign workers.

Restrictions on immigration were added and deportations began. Because of the difficult atmosphere, many Mexicans left of their own volition. Coincidentally, the land reform of President Lázaro Cárdenas (1934–40) made returning to Mexico an attractive option for those who desired to own property. At the same time, the problem of a lack of farm workers in California due to this exodus was resolved by the migration of the Okies to the West Coast. Once more, one people's loss proved to be another's gain.

1941–86. The next important event in US-Mexican labor relations was the 1942 signing of the *bracero* agreement (from the Spanish *brazo*, "arm"). Another world war (and a decade later the Korean War) generated the need for additional manpower, and as always the agricultural sector was short of laborers. The *bracero* program granted visas for temporary contract work. The numbers stipulated in the treaty never satisfied the need, however, and over time undocumented immigration began to grow. In 1954, during a time of suspicion of everything foreign (the McCarthy era), the INS launched "Operation Wetback" in parts of California, Texas, and Arizona. It was designed to apprehend anyone believed to be in the country illegally. Officials claimed that over a million Latin Americans were apprehended. The *bracero* program was eventually shut down in 1965 due in large measure to pressure from union and civil rights groups.[12]

The Immigration and Nationality Act of 1952 preserved the quota system (although the allocations were calculated differently than in the 1924 bill), set standards for labor procurement, and defined qualifications for eligibility for sponsoring family members. It was significantly impacted by new legislation in 1965 (Hart-Cellar Immigration Bill), which reset the limits of permissible entries for any country at a maximum of 20,000. Moreover, a ceiling of 120,000 visas was imposed on the entire Western hemisphere. Mexico, like every other country, was given the 20,000 allotment. This system took effect in 1968, but clearly it was utterly unrealistic in light of the history of Mexican labor in this country. An unexpected, but certainly inevitable, result was an exponential increase in undocumented immigration. The number of legal visas for Mexicans was eventually raised considerably, but it never reached levels to match labor needs. The pressure for migration northward was exacerbated by worsening economic conditions in Mexico and the rapid increase in its population. In other words, while restrictions were growing, more and more people were trying to enter the country to find work.

In response, the Immigration Reform and Control Act (IRCA) was passed by Congress in 1986, during the Reagan administration. This was the most significant piece of legislation since 1965, and it has been the principal tool regulating issues related to immigration for the past two decades. Sectors of the nation were feeling uncomfortable with the growing number of Hispanics because of the cost implications for public services and nativistic concerns. Texas, for example, passed a law excluding Hispanic children of undocumented parents from attending public schools, but this was overturned by the Supreme Court in 1982 (*Plyer vs. Doe*). To control the flow of immigrants from Mexico, IRCA fortified the Border Patrol and developed more procedures and weightier sanctions for employers regarding the hiring of undocumented workers. This law also provided amnesty to those who could prove that they had been in the US since 1982 and to a special category of farm workers. In all, over 3 million applied for amnesty.

This new arrangement, however, did not achieve its intended outcomes. Many employers balked at the amount of required paperwork, while others simply did not want to lose their cheap source of labor. The demand for documentation also spawned a black market in fraudulent papers and encouraged many employers to pay salaries in cash to evade their legal responsibilities. In addition, the

35

preference system for reuniting families allowed those who had received amnesty to bring over their kin; this led to the admission of many more people than the government had anticipated. The resulting emerging Hispanic networks and communities in turn fostered the conditions to receive and help even more immigrants come to the country. In many ways, then, IRCA proved to be counterproductive.

1986–present. Other schemes attempted to respond to these unforeseen problems. The Immigration Act of 1990 increased employer sanctions, strengthened the Border Patrol, made eligibility of family members more difficult, and sought to encourage the entry of people, especially more skilled workers, from more developed countries. The Illegal Immigration Reform and Immigrant Responsibility Act of 1996 (IIRIRA), among other things, funded increased surveillance along the border, limited access to Social Security benefits for undocumented immigrants, and allowed states to reduce public services to immigrants. The Personal Responsibility and Work Opportunity Reconciliation Act of 1996 reinforced the restrictions of IIRIRA and added others.

More recently, there have been several well-publicized attempts to pass comprehensive legislation aimed at providing solutions to the increasingly complex matter of Hispanic immigration. Proposals have come from all sides of the debate, but the potentially most far-reaching have not passed both houses of Congress. For example, the Border Protection, Antiterrorism, and Illegal Immigration Control Act of 2005 (also known as the Sensenbrenner Bill) authorized the construction of seven hundred miles of fencing along the border with Mexico and added more restrictions and sanctions; it was approved by the House of Representatives but did not receive the necessary votes in the Senate. A series of compromise bipartisan bills, which attempted to wed increased border security and enforcement of sanctions with an increase in the number of visas and the provision of an avenue to residency or citizenship, have also failed: in the House, the STRIVE Act of 2007 (Security through Regularized Immigration and a Vibrant Economy Act); in the Senate, the Secure America and Orderly Immigration Act of 2005 (the McCain-Kennedy Bill), the Comprehensive Immigration Reform Act of 2006, and the Comprehensive Immigration Reform Act of 2007 (the Secure Borders, Economic Opportunity, and Immigration Reform Act). The most recent federal legislation has not been approved, at least in part, because the elections of 2008 loom on the horizon. Pressures on the nation's politicians have increased, and not a few are hesitant to anger any of their constituencies. With the latest stalemates in June 2007, it appears as if any new initiatives will have to wait until after the 2008 elections and the installation of the 111th Congress (January 2009).

During the past fifteen years, as the Hispanic presence has become more prominent, a number of initiatives at local and state levels have also attempted to discourage immigration. These have been of several kinds. Some of the more high-profile forms in three areas have been:

- Security: In 1993 Silvestre Reyes, Border Patrol chief in El Paso, Texas, organized Operation Blockade, an intense effort to intercept undocumented immigrants. It was later renamed Operation Hold the Line. Reyes later ran for election to the House of Representatives. Other border programs with similar purposes: Operation Gatekeeper, San Diego, California (1994);[13] Operation Safeguard, Nogales, Arizona (1995); Operation Rio Grande, Brownsville, Texas (1997). Since their initial launching, the reach of these enforcement measures along the border has been extended. All of these strategies increased vigilance by supplementation of patrol personnel, the installation of fences and floodlights, and other defensive measures.

- Restriction of social services, health care, and public education (ballot initiatives): Proposition 187, California (1994; it was declared unconstitutional in 1998).
- English only in public education (ballot initiatives): Many states have passed such legislation. The two most prominent at the national level were Proposition 227 in California (1998) and Proposition 200 in Arizona (2000).

Another layer of confusion and tension involves the coordination between local, state, and federal laws and agencies in relation to permissible regulations and proper jurisdiction.[14] A well-publicized case is the tough law directed against undocumented Hispanic immigrants that was passed in the small Pennsylvania town of Hazleton in July 2006. Citing negative effects on the community's quality of life by the recent arrival of a significant number of immigrants, the city council decreed a series of fines to discourage, among other things, hiring immigrants or renting to them. A federal judge struck down the measure on July 27, 2007, claiming that setting these kinds of laws lay outside the province of local government. The bill had been fought by several advocacy groups. The town plans to appeal the ruling.[15]

Finally, the administration of the border with Mexico has also changed considerably in the past few years. In the wake of the attacks of September 11, 2001, the Department of Homeland Security was established in November 2002. The INS was absorbed into the Department of Homeland Security several months later, in the spring of 2003. Consequently, INS activities and the Border Patrol were folded into the newly formed Immigration and Customs Enforcement Agency (ICE), which is a bureau of the department. Border security has thus become part of the more comprehensive national effort to control terrorism and drug traffic.

This very cursory survey of the history of immigration demonstrates the baffling and contradictory state of affairs in the United States today. The path that brought the country to this point has been anything but consistent or straight. The realities concerning immigration are an unwieldy set of regulations (for the government, employers, the soliciting immigrant, and their families); huge backlogs in processing applications; awkward synchronization between federal agencies and between these and state and local governments; prisons overcrowded with immigrants awaiting trial or deportation; more deaths due to security measures that have driven immigrants to pass through desert regions; conflicts in educational policies; an overburdened health-care system; a deeply divided public among the majority culture; and a Hispanic population that is at once hopeful, timorous, and frustrated. Any solution in the future will have to be as intricately complex as the many facets of the present situation. No legislation can satisfy everyone, nor will it be without its own inherent problems. To unravel the muddle is a tall order and will be messy business. That is the only thing that is certain.

As the country tries to move forward, two central issues continually come to the fore: the question of national identity and the potential economic impact of Hispanic immigration. I will deal with each one of these topics in turn and introduce additional components to each about which readers may be unaware.

Who Are "We"? The Question of National Identity

The Threat to "Americanness"

Demographics.[16] The official government census states that in 2000 there were 35.3 million Hispanics in the United States, a figure that represented 12.5 percent of the total population (the inclusion of Puerto Rico would have added 3.8 million to that number).[17] These statistics also reveal that between 1990 and 2000 the Hispanic population increased by over 50 percent. This rapid growth was due primarily to immigration but also includes a comparatively higher birthrate.[18] As of 2007, Hispanics numbered over 40 million. They presently make up over 14 percent of the national population and are responsible for almost half of the national population growth since 2000. Estimates on how many Hispanics are undocumented range from 12 million to 20 million, the largest percentage being of Mexican origin. Though historically Hispanics migrated primarily to the Southwest (especially to California and Texas), their presence today is truly a national phenomenon. Hispanics have supplanted African-Americans as the largest minority group in the country.

> What will "American" mean in twenty years? Will it even be a relevant term?

What worries many are the possible changes in national character that might result from this significant demographic shift. How might this large influx change the cultural landscape? What will "American" mean in twenty years? Will it even be a relevant term? Will English still be the dominant language? In a recent book, Samuel Huntington (*The Clash of Civilizations*) sounds an alarm.[19] Slowly but surely, he claims, the markers of classic American identity are being buried by millions of new immigrants, especially those from Latin America.

The treasured cultural core includes what Huntington calls America's historic "creed" of liberal democracy, individualism, private property, and the market. These are all important commitments for the people of the United States, but this creed is not ultimately what makes this country unique. The heart of the national identity, he says, is its Anglo-Protestant beliefs and values, the English language, and the legacy of Western European culture.

Cultural assimilation. Huntington claims that, unlike earlier immigrants, new arrivals today are not assimilating at the same rate or with the same conviction to leave behind their original national identity. In fact, they seem reluctant to do so, and several factors actually work against their assimilation. The immigration from Latin America is different from previous periods in several ways. To begin with, the Mexican border is contiguous with the United States. The home country is not an ocean away, as it would have been for those coming from Europe a century ago. Entry and movement back and forth between north and south are therefore much easier, so fewer feel the need to adapt to the mores and language of the host country. In addition, the sheer quantity of Hispanic immigrants dwarfs anything in history. They are also persistent. Neither failure to make it past border patrols nor deportation back to their countries of origin are sufficient deterrents to discourage them from trying again and again. Third, these immigrants tend to concentrate in certain parts of the country and live within enclaves in those areas, thereby slowing down their integration into the larger society.

Evidence of this lack of assimilation, according to Huntington, is found in declining levels of English language acquisition, less educational achievement, and poorer socioeconomic success. There also is a lack of enthusiasm, he says, to seek American citizenship in comparison with immigrant groups from other parts of the world. Hispanics appear to want to maintain their language, their customs, and even their foreign citizenship, even as they take advantage of the new way of life afforded by their work here. The disinclination to accept this country's historical culture and to forswear their national allegiances is abetted by certain sectors of academia, the media, and political elites as part of a defense of multiculturalism. The efforts of these groups seriously compound the problem of the slow pace or even the possibility of assimilation.

Other prominent figures echo Huntington's concerns and agree with his negative assessment of multiculturalism and its role in impeding the assimmilation process. Victor Davis Hanson relates how his home state of California has changed in the past two decades, sliding toward a conversion into what he creatively labels "Mexifornia." In his view, legislators, educators, and other activists have fostered an attitude of victimization among Hispanics and have sanctioned the separation of races—a new form of tribalism—all of which makes the governance of the state more difficult and has brought California to the brink of financial disaster. The very things about this country that would have drawn Mexicans and other Latin Americans here in the first place, such as participation in a vibrant economy and educational achievement with all of the horizons it can open, are being cordoned off. The result, Hanson says, is that the life immigrants lead can often be a sad cycle of despair in which they navigate the dark underside of illegality. Of course, business people, who continue to offer jobs to immigrants and pay little, perpetuate the quagmire.

Colorado Congressman Tom Tancredo and syndicated columnist and news show pundit Pat Buchanan are more shrill in their tone.[20] The titles of their books, *In Mortal Danger* and *State of Emergency*, respectively, veritably shout gloom and doom.[21] Like Hanson, these authors underscore the damaging impact on public services and education and decry bilingualism. They emphasize, too, the activities of brutal Hispanic gangs (in particular the Mara Salvatrucha or M-13) and the escalation of drug trafficking along the border. Tancredo connects Hispanic immigration to concerns for post 9/11 security and claims that terrorists ("Islamofacists") are slipping through the porous boundary with Mexico. Buchanan goes so far as to argue that a concerted *reconquista* (the retaking by peaceful means of what formally was part of Mexico) is under way, masterminded by Mexican government officials and elites.

Hispanic voices. Some high profile Hispanics have presented their lives, at least to some degree, as testimonies to significant assimilation to the majority culture, in particular with respect to the learning of English and the ideal of educational advancement. One of the better known is the former director of the US Commission on Civil Rights, neoconservative Linda Chávez. Another, but from a very different ideological perspective, is the editorialist Richard Rodríguez. Both believe ethnic issues should be dealt with in the private realm because in the public sector they are more likely to take the form of sociopolitical constructs than to be a reflection of reality. Yet in neither case has the road been uncomplicated or without personal cost. Chávez has been sharply criticized by certain Hispanic activists and others for her assimilationist opinions on such matters; at the same time, she has been viciously attacked for stating that she believes that racism lies behind some of the anti-immigrant feelings in this country.[22] Rodríguez is dismissive of what he characterizes as tangled thinking regarding the notion of "Hispanic," yet he has written an eloquent trilogy that traces the difficult path he traveled to arrive at his own stance.[23]

Hispanics and the Identity Predicament

Are these worries about the possible harm to national identity legitimate? Are they a fair appraisal of the cultural landscape? Can more restrictive measures preserve "Americanness"? On the one hand, increased controls on undocumented immigrants serve to isolate that group in many ways. Ironically, then, they keep these Hispanics from incorporating themselves fully into national life, or at the very least slow that process down. They help ensure that the identity complaint becomes a self-fulfilling prophecy. On the other hand, careful reflection from a broader point of reference reveals that issues surrounding identity are more multifaceted than simply the majority culture's anxiety over the loss of what it considers to be its central values and way of life.

Hispanics elsewhere. To begin with, unease about a surge in Hispanic immigration is not limited to the United States. In recent years Hispanics have also been migrating to Europe. As is the case in this country, issues related to *coyotes* and immigrant safety and rights, potential economic effects, and national identity are the discussion points in public discourse and political planning.[24] In a paradoxical reversal of history, the nations of Europe that in the past experienced the emigration of millions of their own to other places are today a destination for immigrants.

The movement from Latin America has been going on for some time, and tougher legal restrictions and greater difficulties for entering into the US have increased migration across the Atlantic Ocean. Spain is a case in point. It is a remarkable case, too, because there are many commonalities between that "Mother Country" and the Spanish-speaking nations that historically were its colonies. In Spain, even while low birth rates and a budding economy in fact require the absorption of a large number of newcomers, racial tensions are rising and new restrictive laws are being put into place.[25] The cultural fears felt in the Untied States, then, are natural emotions for any host country. They also fit into the nativistic patterns, mentioned earlier, that have recurred throughout the nation's history. But is the concern for identity limited to the majority culture? Should the discussion of cultural identity be reconfigured and expanded?

Hispanic identity. Clearly, Hispanics in the United States are wrestling with identity, too. They are struggling with who they are and what they might become in the inescapable processes of cultural adaptation. Like most immigrants, Hispanics have to become acquainted with and live in unfamiliar settings while removed from their social and kinship networks and support. They wonder how they are to raise their children with the positive values of Latin American culture that sometimes clash with those of North American consumerism and individualism. Love of their home country and culture pull at their heart strings. There are also the contradictory emotions over the well-being of family members left behind and the pressure to send money back to help, even as immigrants strive to make a go of life here.

For many younger Hispanics arriving today and those of the second and third generation, however, the primary issue is no longer learning how to navigate a strange system to find work. Allegiance to the country and culture of their parents is not the same. The challenge is deeper and focused elsewhere. The United States is now more home than a target destination; it is not just the land of opportunity for a better paying job. Every dimension of life as a minority must be negotiated with the world that surrounds them: skin color, the language of the home and language of the public sphere, accents, slang, music, religion, social status, cultural rituals (like the *quinceañera*), food, sports, and fashion styles. The crucial point is that the very fact that this give and take is happening is ample proof that *assimilation is taking place.*[26]

This complicated set of changes and redefinitions has become the focus of multiple sociological and anthropological studies that probe how immigrants live their lives "over here" and what "back there" comes to mean over time. Some of the titles are captivating (*From Cuenca to Queens* by Ann Miles), others revealing (*Mexican New York* by Robert Courtney Smith). This research reveals that multiple factors, such as modern technology, economic globalization, and the mobility of people, are producing cultural and linguistic hybrids and multiple loyalties that are part of a phenomenon called "transnationalism."[27] In other words, the acquisition of English and other assimilation benchmarks that the majority culture might have are not straightforward bullet points on a checklist. Hispanics are learning the language at a steady pace and adapting in many ways, but there is a whole constellation of processes occurring concurrently at home (the

45

home in the US and the home in the native country), the workplace, church, school, and the shopping mall.[28]

The pain of becoming and understanding a different identity mix is a constant theme of Hispanic literature. Works by novelists who have roots in both North America and south of the border, such as Francisco Goldman (Guatemala), Sandra Cisneros and Victor Villaseñor (Mexico), Edmundo Paz Soldán (Bolivia), and Julia Álvarez (Dominican Republic), depict the conflicts of heart and mind of the immigrant or descendent vis-à-vis their Latin American heritage and their life in the United States. With a beauty and an intricacy worthy of their topic, these writers explore the strain felt in being somewhere and nowhere at the same time, in feeling the struggle between the memories and traces of before and the realities of the moment, in living in that in-between place within their adopted country and with ties to their homeland—all of this very difficult to articulate, but so authentic, so agonizing to the soul.[29]

Cisneros closes her magnificent work *Caramelo or Puro Cuento* with a lament of her main character, Celaya ("Lala") Reyes. Lala has come to the realization that she cannot integrate easily into Mexico City, but neither can she fit neatly into San Antonio or Chicago. At this point in her life the multiple pieces of culture, family, and country that reside deeply within her are too hard to reconcile into a coherent whole:

> And I don't know how it is with anyone else, but for me these things, that song, that time, that place, are all bound together in a country I am homesick for, that doesn't exist anymore. They never existed. A country I invented. Like all emigrants caught between here and there.[30]

There is angst, but there is also the sense of growing into another kind of person—although that is not yet defined for her at the moment. Living "in the hyphen" (Mexican-

46

American, Cuban-American, etc.) is a pilgrimage of joy and sadness, of frustration and self-discovery, of appreciation for the past and anticipation of the future.

The reaction of other Hispanics to this dilemma, in contrast, has been to celebrate the fact of difference. The initial coming together of races and cultures in what is now Latin America occurred centuries ago, when the Spanish came to the New World and conquered the indigenous peoples. That first blending of blood, symbolized forever in Latin American lore in the relationship between the *conquistador* Hernán Cortés and the Aztec woman Malintzín ("La Malinche"), produced the first *mestizos* (those of mixed race). Later would come the amalgamation with Africans (most of whom were brought over as slaves) in the Caribbean and along the Atlantic coastline, and with European settlers. Hispanics are the heirs of this grand *mestizaje* (mixture) in all of its richness and variety.[31] There is great worth in this legacy that many simply are not aware of. Some activists use this distinctive heterogeneous identity as a rallying cry against any degradation they feel victimizes Hispanics; *mestizaje* allows them to stand up to the majority culture with pride. Such a reaction is not surprising, but another constructive means of appreciating this concept is possible.

The inevitable convergence of this Hispanic diversity and the majority culture can be interpreted as yet another chapter in the ongoing historical process of *mestizaje*. New combinations are being born of both cultures, as each mutually enriches and energizes the other. The result will be unexpected variations for the common good. Each cultural mix brings unique gifts (and weaknesses, too), but in the end the metamorphosis will benefit all.[32] This is not romantic optimism. I am aware of the many difficulties and the great discomfort inherent in this transformation, but I am also convinced that change is certain and that it will be fruitful.

The future of national identity. Whence identity or, perhaps better, identities? The United States is in the midst of a transition time, and that inexorable renovation is unavoidably awkward and often painful—for all parties. But then again the American identity has never been a static entity. It has meant different things at diverse times, as millions from all over the world have come to this country and have added their part. African-Americans were forcefully kept from the cultural mainstream for the longest time, first as slaves and later as a despised minority. The Civil War and civil rights legislation were not enough to guarantee that those Americans could become part of, let alone participate in defining, the national identity. That singular process is still ongoing and uneven. With Hispanic immigration, American life is being reshaped again.

> The United States is in the midst of a transition time, and that inexorable renovation is unavoidably awkward and often painful—for all parties.

The metaphor of the "melting pot" is an idea that is regularly bantered about in discussions about assimilation. A flaw in the metaphor, as commonly understood, is that it can convey the notion that, as new elements are brought in, things essentially remain the same. Besides the tricky problem of determining who should define what the "same" is and what its boundaries are, there are at least two mistaken ideas of this conception of the melting-pot model. First, history contradicts the belief that there is some fixed cultural and linguistic core that has endured unchanged over long periods of time. The facts say otherwise. Second, the adaptation process for host country or immigrant is never easy or neutral precisely because it is not a natural turning back to or a conversion to some pristine essence. It is a melding together of a minority into and within the majority culture, but the end product is unpredictable and open ended. It has always been so. These developments are an opportunity for an enhancement of national identity, not a threat to be warded off at all costs.[33]

Economic Realities: What Does Hispanic Immigration Cost?

In addition to the arguments over cultural impact, discussions also revolve around the economics of immigration. That is, disagreements arise over the actual and potential costs and benefits of Hispanic immigration. Do local, state, and federal tax revenues generated by immigrants outweigh the amount of money required for their health care, education, law enforcement, and welfare? Should the money gathered from taxes be the sole indicator of revenue? Is it enough to consider economic issues only from the perspective of what is happening within the United States, or are they part of global economic realities?

The Impact on Jobs and Public Services

Basic complaints. Tom Tancredo presents in popular fashion four of the economic arguments commonly used to promote a more restrictive immigration policy.[34] He contends, to begin with, that the children of undocumented immigrants are an added financial burden on local school systems. New programs must be crafted to meet their special needs, such as English as a second language. This, in turn, requires hiring more teachers and translates into greater expense for additional classrooms, supplies, and utilities. Increased numbers also create the necessity of providing extra meals and transportation. Second, among these immigrants are many criminals, and the cost of their incarceration is crippling the prison system. Third, the fact that immigrants are willing to accept below-average wages drives down the income of American citizens. As the market adjusts to this lower pay scale, legal workers are forced to accept less than their proper due. Last, Tancredo contends, health care is being adversely affected by the presence of undocumented immigrants. Hospitals legally

49

cannot turn away patients from emergency services, even if they cannot pay for treatment. Hospitals and ultimately state governments have to absorb the unpaid expenses. As a result, emergency rooms around the country are closing down because they are no longer financially viable.

To these four points could be added others. Among them is the contention that the revenue gained from sales taxes on the purchases made by undocumented Hispanics, the property taxes on their residences, and the Social Security contributions and state and federal taxes paid by a certain percentage of these immigrants do not offset the costs listed in the preceding paragraph. Another is that the billions of dollars ($45 billion in 2006)[35] sent as remittances to the families of immigrants (both legal and undocumented) in Latin American are a net loss to the US economy.

The restrictive policy position has its popularizers, but it also has sophisticated advocates. Think tanks and organizations such as the Center for Immigration Studies, the Federation for American Immigration Reform (FAIR), and the Heritage Foundation conduct research on immigration and then make this information available on their Web sites.[36] For those who desire to delve deeper, there are more scholarly publications written by experts or based on academic conferences. These tend to present a more nuanced overview of the present situation than sometimes is available in material geared to a broader audience.

One example would be the issue of the cost of social services.[37] Several variables need to be understood to fully grasp the present state of affairs. First, it is important to be aware that local, state, and federal governments have different sets of expenditures, depending on the programs used by immigrants. In addition, the cost to state governments depends on the number and kinds of programs available to the immigrant and the generosity of their benefits. Other fundamental variables include the size of the immigration population relative to the general population and the kinds of tax revenues that are collected (for instance, is there a state income tax?). These factors differ state by state, so the fiscal effects of the utilization of services by immigrants vary across the country.

Policy alternatives. Proposed policy options (I am avoiding the views of the reactionary fringe) that might respond to the financial challenges are directed at both internal and external realities. Internal measures would involve, for instance, placing more pressure on employers not to hire undocumented immigrants. External measures include regulating the flow of people across the border. This is accomplished by physical means (the wall along the border, patrols, etc.) and by developing different admission policies that would define types of immigrants and how many in each category could be admitted. One proposal is to make entry skill-based, targeting the better educated and more highly trained instead of leaving the door open to the poor and less-academically qualified.[38] The idea is that competent folk could contribute more in taxes because they would receive a higher income; for that very reason, these are likely to employ fewer public services and would be able to pay for any they might use. Another option is to gear the number of permits (both long-term and temporary) to the specific annual needs of agricultural, manufacturing, and service industries. This figure would change year by year and immigrant quotas would adjust accordingly.

Immigration and the Global Economy

Alternative research. Those who argue for policies more favorable to the undocumented immigrant dispute the data and analyses of those of the restrictive persuasion.[39] They respond to each of the points raised above. For instance, a more open position emphasizes that the economic impact of undocumented immigrants cannot be limited to tax revenues and service costs. Taking into account the

51

billions of dollars of Hispanic consumer spending and the many different kinds of industries sustained by Hispanic labor yields a very different economic evaluation, one that supports the notion that Hispanic immigration actually contributes to the national well-being. What is more, the rate of incarceration is much lower among Hispanics than the general population. All social groups of any size have a percentage that will be criminal; this is unavoidable and expected. The fact that the percentage is significantly less than among those who are native-born should discourage unfair stereotyping of immigrants.

Other important issues are also brought to the table. I cite only two. One is that to sustain the Social Security system there is a pressing need for a huge influx of taxable younger workers. Demographic projections of the aging native population indicate that the system cannot continue much longer without a large new revenue source. This need is one argument for the legalization of undocumented immigrants so that all these workers, without exception, pay into the system. Second, employment studies point out that some of the fastest growing occupational categories will be in the service industry, which employs sizeable numbers of unskilled labor in jobs that do not require a high level of education. Not only is the native-born labor force getting older, it is also becoming more educated. On both counts it cannot meet the nation's future labor requirements, but this is precisely the niche that many immigrants can and do fill.

I mention these counterpoints without further detail. They are crucial for a more informed point of view that can respond to the overly negative perceptions of Hispanic immigration. It is enough for my purposes, though, to make readers aware of several of these points of contention in the economic debate. My intent, as in the case of national identity, is to direct attention elsewhere, beyond the usual boundaries of discussion.

It is natural to focus attention on the multiple economic effects immigration has on the host country, in this case the United States. But also to be considered is its impact on the sending, or home, country. What is more, remittances (the movement of capital) and immigration (the migration of labor) are components of the modern global economy.

Remittances. Let us begin with the issue of remittances. In 2006 Guatemala received $3.6 billion in remittances.[40] On the positive side of the ledger, with this money families can improve their housing situation and their general economic status. With the increased cash, there is more consumer spending, which helps the local and national economy in many ways. The impact is evident not only in metropolitan areas, but also in the countryside. One can see the difference these funds have made, for instance, in the highlands. It is not difficult to guess which families have members in the US. The house is now made of concrete block, not adobe. It will often have a second story and a small store at street level. The money, in other words, has been invested in improvements and used to start a small business. Many immigrants not only help their families, they also contribute to community projects such as roads and park maintenance in their villages and towns. In fact, one of the topics of discussion in international development is how governments might be able to direct a certain portion of these funds for community improvement. El Salvador already has a matching funds program in place to encourage contributions from expatriates.

But there also is a negative aspect to the millions of dollars pouring into the Guatemalan economy. The quantity fluctuates according to changes in the US economy, such as the construction industry, and according to the political climate. When anti-immigrant sentiment is high, the flow of remittances drops. The Guatemalan government is also aware that over time remittances inevitably will decrease.

It is now working to create other job opportunities at home and find other sources of outside revenue (increased tourism, foreign investments, etc.). In addition, the loss of labor to the US has lowered agriculture and industry indicators, and in some cases the incentive to work has been adversely affected. (If it is possible to receive more in remittances than what can be earned in the fields and factories, why work?) The presence of hard currency has made prices rise and the cost of land go up; it has also maintained the exchange rate of the national currency, the *quetzal*, at an unrealistic level. The trek north of the father and/or sons sometimes puts acute pressure on the family members left behind (wives, grandparents, children) to meet daily needs without the presence of wage-earning males. For those whose move has not gone well, the loans taken out or the properties mortgaged to pay the *coyote* and other expenses now become a terrible financial burden to the family in Guatemala.

The remittances, in other words, are both blessing and bane. The point is that the economics of Hispanic immigration has wider implications than just what occurs within the United States. For good or ill, *all* of the Americas—North, Central, and South—are invested in the remittances. We need to move beyond the simplistic rhetoric of much of the national debate. Whatever policy is chosen will affect the economies and social well-being of the entire hemisphere. And, if things go badly in Latin America, the ripple effect back to the US would be disastrous. This is a reality one must accept in a global economy.

Global migrant labor. At an even broader level, the migration of labor is a worldwide phenomenon. International economic agreements are coming to grips with the inescapable effect of globalization. This was an unforeseen consequence in some cases and is now becoming a discussion point in newer developments.[41]

One illustration of this is the North American Free Trade Agreement (NAFTA) between the US, Canada, and Mexico, which was launched in 1994. NAFTA's principal purpose was to free up the flow of capital, manufactured goods, and services among these countries. What has become increasingly obvious is that it is not realistic to expect goods and services to move freely (with the lowering of production costs and consumer prices as one of the expectations) and not anticipate labor to move across borders as well. The loss of manufacturing jobs in the US due to the transfer of production to other countries has fueled internal migration by native-born workers in search of new employment and a better life. The same is happening in Latin America. In the case of Mexico, the impact of NAFTA has been mixed. There have been massive job losses, especially in the agricultural sector, and the country is losing the manufacturing battle with other countries, such as China. Mexican labor, therefore, has journeyed northward, looking for work and a better life for their families. This is a human response, and it is worldwide.[42]

The migration of labor—of skilled and unskilled, temporary and more permanent workers—has been an important topic in other international negotiations. The General Agreement on Trade in Services (a treaty of the World Trade Organization—WTO) and the Doha Developmental Round of negotiations of 2001–7 (which was sponsored by the WTO) both include the movement of labor as an agenda item. The Doha Round, whatever its shortcomings, had been organized to design agreements that ideally would benefit primarily developing countries. Its advocates viewed these talks as an expression of the moral obligation of more powerful nations to help move the entire world forward toward greater economic growth and social stability. The economic challenges related to labor were one dimension of this duty.

These larger economic realities show that, while the present debate must deal with the close-at-hand impact of Hispanic immigration, it will not do to leave the discussion at a purely national level. A much wider set of dynamics is at work that needs to be recognized and factored in. The United States is part of a world economy. The workings of global capitalism are affecting financial realities here and abroad in multiple ways, good and bad, and they are all interconnected. The migration of labor is part of this tapestry. And this is a very large piece of cloth indeed, one that is infinitely complex.

The Ignored Dimension: Christian Faith and Hispanics

Hopefully, it is now evident that the historical, cultural, and economic topics that fuel so much rhetoric in this country are much more intricate than many suppose. The backdrop for a more informed discussion will consider the long trajectory of how we got to where we are today and will include an appreciation of the very broad cultural and economic realities that make up Hispanic immigration.

There is still another facet of life that needs to be mentioned, and it can lead to an even fuller understanding of the current scene. This dimension is religion—more specifically, the Christian faith. This important piece of Hispanic identity rarely appears in the national debate. This omission is odd because all who know something of the history and culture of Latin America are well aware that it is an overwhelmingly religious continent. Most Hispanics arrive in the United States with some type of Christian background and awareness.

The New Pulse in Christian Churches

Hispanic Christianity. Christian faith is vibrant among the immigrant population, which now numbers in the millions.[43] The first and most obvious indication of the presence of Hispanic Christians is the increase in the numbers of attendees in churches on a Sunday morning. The face of North American Catholicism is changing, and the church is growing. Masses in parishes around the country are burgeoning with recent arrivals from south of the border (a little more than two-thirds of first generation Hispanic immigrants are Catholic). Estimates place the number of Hispanic Protestant congregations of all stripes in the United States in the many thousands. Mainline denominations, but especially evangelical and Pentecostal denominations and independent groups, are seeing new churches sprout up everywhere. These congregations meet in basements and fellowship halls of existing Anglo churches, in storefronts, and in homes; some have acquired their own facilities. Church size can range from small assemblies of a few dozen worshipers to those where thousands gather together. Associations of pastors and leaders are being organized, the most prominent being the evangelical National Hispanic Christian Leadership Conference. The National Hispanic Prayer Breakfast is now an annual event in Washington DC.

> Christian faith is vibrant among the immigrant population, which now numbers in the millions.

The landscape of Hispanic Christianity is as diverse as Hispanic culture, and this variety makes any sort of simplistic generalizations impossible. Some features, though, are worth pointing out. For instance, Hispanic Catholicism is influenced by the popular (sometimes syncretistic), communal, and celebratory faith of the Americas.[44] The Virgin of Guadalupe and the saints are much more important than in Anglo-Catholicism. Easter week processions, *posadas* at Christmas time, and other traditional observances are beginning to appear. Interestingly, over half of Hispanic Catholics classify themselves as charismatic.

In many places Pentecostals make up the majority of Protestant Hispanic churches and usually have the largest congregations.[45] Some of these churches belong to the historic Pentecostal denominations such as the Assemblies of God and the Church of God, Cleveland. Others are mission churches planted by Latin American neo-Pentecostal denominations. In metro-Denver I know of several groups whose mother churches are in Guatemala: Iglesia Elim, El Shaddai, and Palabra en Acción. There are also those that began here and do not have formal connections with any organization. These Pentecostal and neo-Pentecostal churches have their own particular flavor: exuberance and joy in worship, a reverence for the Bible, a strong commitment to evangelism, an interest in the last days, and in some cases the celebration of a gospel of prosperity and healing. In addition, some Hispanic denominational churches manifest configurations that are different from their majority-culture counterparts. One can find Baptists with a more vibrant tone, and congregations of mainline churches might have Pentecostal touches and an interest in evangelism and Bible study that normally are associated with evangelicalism.

In addition to functioning as sanctuaries for worship, Hispanic churches can serve as networking centers for finding jobs and helping those in need; some work to connect immigrants to appropriate resources for getting their legal matters straightened out. Congregations may also take on the role of the extended family of Latin American culture. It is not uncommon to see Hispanic churches meeting together in a park on a Sunday afternoon, sharing the meal and warmth that would have been reserved for Sunday gatherings at a relative's house in their "former life." In some instances in the past and increasingly more in the present, churches have mobilized for social and political causes.[46]

Hispanic ministries. The Catholic Church and many Protestant denominations see this explosion in the number of churches and churchgoers as an unprecedented opportunity for all kinds of pastoral and caring ministries. It has also led to the establishment of training institutions all over the country. The Catholic Church, Protestant denominations, and several seminaries have begun programs at different educational levels to help meet the need for equipped laity and pastors for this burgeoning Christian body. In the past two decades the number of Hispanic persons with graduate degrees has been on the rise. There are now professional organizations for Hispanic theologians, such as ACTHUS (Academy of Catholic Theologians of the United States) and AETH (Asociación para la Educación Teológica Hispana), and several academic theological journals. English-speaking publishing houses of a breadth of persuasions have begun to publish works in English by these theologians or have incorporated a Spanish wing (sometimes by acquiring Latin American publishers). One could also mention the proliferation of recording labels for gospel singers of all styles of music, glossy magazines with different target audiences, youth conventions and rallies, and seminars for pastors and lay people focusing on a wide variety of topics of interest.

All of these are elements of a fast growing Christian Hispanic culture that is as multifaceted and diverse in its beliefs and activities as that of the majority Christian culture—albeit with its own distinctive flavor. This phenomenon is not just something to be aware of or to be considered simply a new target for outreach; it contains perspectives that have much to teach majority culture Christians and their churches about life with God. Both Christian cultures have much to learn from each other.[47]

In speaking of Hispanic immigration, therefore, one must be aware that with this movement of millions have come countless believers and that many others are coming to faith after they arrive in the United States. For the Christian, Hispanic immigration can no longer be conceived as an anonymous mass of people or reduced to arguments over statistics. Many immigrants are brothers and sisters in Christ, with all the respect and attention this fact should engender in those of the majority culture who claim to love and follow Jesus.

The "Browning" of Christianity

This spiritual and ecclesiological appreciation of Hispanic immigration can be broadened still further by placing it within the context of changes in the profile of Christianity at the global level. During the past one hundred years, Roman Catholicism and Protestantism of all stripes have experienced explosive growth in Africa, Asia, and Latin America. The greater part of Christians now live outside North America and Western Europe. Some characterize this movement of Christianity's center of gravity as the "browning" or "globalizing" of the faith.

Philip Jenkins is one who has charted this population shift and its increasing effect on the face of Christianity. In his book *The Next Christendom*, he describes the vibrant energy of groups from the southern hemisphere.[48] Jenkins highlights their belief in the supernatural and healing, fresh worship styles, concern for social justice, and robust commitment to evangelism. This especially typifies evangelical and Pentecostal churches, which are the fastest growing groups. Another trait Jenkins focuses on, which he has developed more fully in a newer work, is a strong adherence to the Bible.[49] These believers are overwhelmingly a people of the Book, people who cherish the Scriptures. What often distinguishes them on a Sunday morning is that they carry a Bible under their arm. They gladly memorize passages, devote themselves to biblical study, and try to apply its teachings to all areas of life with the profound conviction of its immediacy and relevance. Of course, these very same characteristics also pertain to many Hispanic churches in the United States, whose members are part of this global phenomenon.

Still another feature of this incarnation of the Christian faith is its missionary spirit. The global South has become

60

a launching pad for a fresh missionary movement, with countries such as Nigeria and South Korea leading the way in commissioning missionaries and establishing missionary training centers and agencies. From its inception, Christianity has been a mobile faith, always on the move, always sending out messengers of the Word into new areas and planting churches on virgin soil. As a result, the demographic, administrative, and educational hub of the Christian faith has shifted progressively over time from the eastern Mediterranean to Europe to the United States, and now to several locations in the South. In the past few decades and still more in the years to come, Berlin, London, New York City, Chicago, Wheaton, Colorado Springs, and Los Angeles will give way to Nairobi, Seoul, São Paulo, Guatemala City, and other metropolises in the Two-Thirds World.[50]

What does this seismic shift in Christianity have to do with Hispanic immigration? The answer lies in appreciating the breadth and power of what God is doing in the world today. The zeal of this "next Christendom" finds expression in the many organized efforts on the part of institutions in the South to propagate the faith around the world. At the same time, the spread of this fresh wave of Christianity is occurring by means of the migration of millions of believers to other lands. From this perspective, could what we are witnessing in this country be part of a divinely directed global phenomenon? Is God bringing millions of Hispanics to the United States to revitalize the Christian churches here and to present to those who do not yet believe the opportunity to turn to Christ in their search for a new life? Many Hispanics and pastors sincerely believe that God has led them here for a purpose: to play an important role in a revival of the Christian faith in this country.

In other words, if Christians of the majority culture take a very different look at Hispanic immigration, they will see that something much bigger than they might have imagined is happening. The church of Jesus Christ is growing

61

and being impacted in unexpected ways. This work of God is part of an enormous movement that spans the globe.

Conclusion

In the introduction I stated that the title *Christians at the Border* has a literal and a metaphorical dimension. This chapter has offered a long reflection on the literal dividing line between the United States and Mexico that runs from the Gulf of Mexico to the Pacific Ocean. We have looked at the history of Hispanic immigration and then probed two of the most hotly contested topics: national identity and economic impact. In each case my goal has been to demonstrate just how complicated these issues are. They are unbelievably multifaceted. The last section added still another piece to the complex puzzle: the presence of millions of Hispanic Christians.

This more realistic picture of what constitutes Hispanic immigration should give everyone pause. If one is a Christian, whether of the majority culture or Hispanic, it compels one to seek the wisdom of God. For many of us the ultimate source for this wisdom is the Bible. For that reason, the next three chapters will examine how this divine Word might shed light on the national debate. Accounts in the Bible of the migration of people are pervasive, and there is a constant emphasis on displaying appropriate attitudes to the outsider. The amount of biblical material relevant to immigrational issues today may prove to be surprising.

The contention of this book is this: if Christians want to address the problems posed by the immigration of Hispanic peoples and contribute to possible solutions, then they should do so consciously *as Christians* and more specifically *as biblically informed Christians*.

2

OF IMMIGRANTS, REFUGEES, AND EXILES

Guidance from the Old Testament, Part I

I have poor eyesight. For many, many years I have worn bifocals. I cannot see either close up or far away without help. The computer age has complicated my situation. I have to have a separate pair of eyeglasses for working with my laptop because the screen sits in that intermediate space that neither part of the bifocal can handle well. What is worse, if I want to read the small print on a label, I have to take off my glasses altogether and bring the writing up close to make out the words! Without any of these lenses I can still see—even if everything is a bit blurred. But I am not blind. Once I put on my glasses, things become clear.

In like manner, all of us have a certain way of looking at ourselves and the world in which we live. Every one of us, in other words, has a particular set of lenses through which we interpret the reality that surrounds us and our identity and role in that context. These lenses are calibrated according to our background and experiences. But for the Christian, the Bible can serve as a different and fresh set of lenses. As the Word of God, it should profoundly shape our vision of life. The Bible is the set of lenses that brings us and everything around us into focus as God would want us to perceive them. This view of the world may be at odds with the way others regard matters, but the important point is that through the Bible we as believers gain proper perspective, the angle God desires we have on important issues.

This chapter and the two that follow probe what the Bible has to say about matters related to immigration. This information can be part of the lenses that enable Christians—both those of the majority culture and Hispanics—to process issues related to immigration in the United States today. This survey is not exhaustive, nor is it a technical exercise in biblical scholarship.[1] My goal is to demonstrate the breadth of relevant material in the Bible in order to remind all concerned that God has much to teach all of us. Some of what follows comes from Hispanic biblical studies that can shed new light on passages in ways that might surprise the reader.[2]

A Growing Concern

As the presence of Hispanics continues to grow, a variety of church bodies have begun to address immigration from an overt faith perspective. Different denominations and organizations have also made official pronouncements with respect to immigration (see the list in the appendix). Additional materials are beginning to appear in journals, books, and on the Internet. The Catholic Church, in contrast to most, has a long tradition of including the migrant in its pastoral concerns. The right to migrate is connected to the church's call to care for the vulnerable on the one hand, and to the entitlement to dignity and the responsibility of providing for family on the other. There is a history of teaching that spans, for example, from Pope Pius XII's *Exsul Familia* in 1952 to Pope John Paul II's 1999 *Ecclesia in America* (paragraph 65) and his various messages on World Migration Day, the 2004 Instruction *Erga migrantes caritas Christi*, and the declarations of the recent Fifth General Conference of Latin American and Caribbean Bishops that was celebrated with Pope Benedict XVI in Brazil in May 2007 (CELAM, *Documento de Aparecida*, paragraphs 411–16).[3] These statements and more extensive studies sometimes reference a few passages in the Old and New Testaments. Much, though, has been left unsaid.

> What it means to be a human must be the foundation for any discussion.

This overview of what the Bible has to say about immigration begins at the beginning, as it were—in the book of Genesis—with the creation of man and woman in the image of God. What it means to be a human must be the foundation for any discussion. The chapter then discusses the many people of God in the Old Testament who for all kinds of reasons had to leave their home country and settle somewhere else. Migration is not a new phenomenon; it is as old as time. Chapter 3 discusses the virtue of hospitality in Old Testament times and the various laws in the Pentateuch regarding foreigners. Chapter 4 turns attention to the New Testament.

The Image of God

Genesis 1

Above all else, immigration is the movement of *people* across borders. The bottom line is that it concerns humans:

65

their worth, destiny, rights, and responsibilities. The Bible gives great prominence to the creation of humans. Their creation is the climax of the account of Genesis 1. It is the last step in the divine movement to organize the chaos and fill the emptiness of the new world. In the narrative, the first three days of creation involve dividing darkness from light; separating the land, water, and sky; and preparing the earth for habitation (Gen. 1:3–13). On the fourth, fifth, and sixth days God places celestial bodies in the heavens, fish in the sea, and birds in the sky (vv. 14–25). The final piece of his handiwork is the creation of man and woman (vv. 26–31).

Six times the text says that God saw what he had made and that it was "good" (1:4, 10, 12, 18, 21, 25). Everything was in its proper place and functioning as it should under the sovereignty of the Creator; the whole scene teems with sanctified life. After the creation of humans, the text declares, "and it was *very* good" (v. 31). Fittingly, this is the seventh occurrence of the term "good." Seven is a special number in the Bible and regularly represents perfection. The qualifier "very good" and the number seven together emphasize that the creation of people is the pinnacle of what God has made. Humans are special indeed.

What is it, though, that makes humans unique among the other living creatures in the created order? Verses 26 and 27 teach that every person, male and female, is made in the image of God. What does this concept of the image of God actually mean? How might this truth about humanity inform the immigration debate?

There are at least three views as to what it means to be created in the image of God.[4] The first argues that the image deals with what humans *inherently are* or *possess*. The idea is that every person has a will, intellect, emotions, and a spiritual component that distinguish them from all other creatures. Others take the position that the image should be considered *relationally*. Those who take this position believe that the only person who ever truly incarnated the image of God was Jesus (2 Cor. 4:4; Col. 1:15). Individuals who are reconciled with God through faith in him are able to participate in the image and thus regain the relationship with God that was ruptured at the fall in Genesis 3. Finally, some contend that the image of God ought to be understood in a *functional* sense. In the ancient world, kings would set up statues of themselves in far-off territories as a witness to their authority over that region. In like manner, humans, who are God's image on earth, are designed to represent him here. This representation is not to be passive; men and women are to preside over all things as God's vice regents (Gen. 1:26, 28). This dominion requires wisdom, creativity, and care, and God has splendidly equipped every human for this great task.

Each of these three perspectives has a biblical basis (although the last seems to be the one most clearly stressed in Genesis 1). Each one in its own way underscores the particular value of all persons: what they inherently are, their potential relationship with the Creator, and their capacity and privilege as rulers. Everyone is made in God's image and therefore has a singular standing before God and in the world.

Implications for Today

Value as persons. The creation of all persons in the image of God must be the most basic conviction for Christians as they approach the challenges of immigration today. Immigration should not be argued in the abstract because it is fundamentally about *immigrants.* Immigrants are humans, and as such they are made in God's image. Each and every one of those who have come to the United States is God's creation and is worthy of respect. Because immigrants are made in the divine image, they have an essential value and possess the potential to contribute to society through their presence, work, and ideas.

Human rights and the image of God. If one takes what the Bible says in Genesis 1 seriously, as revelation from God, then what it communicates about humans becomes a divine claim on Christian attitudes and actions toward those who have arrived in this country—irrespective of whether they are here with or without the documents the government might mandate. To turn away or to treat badly one made in the image of God ultimately is a violation against God. As a consequence, the topic of immigration at some level needs to be considered from a human rights perspective and not be defined solely in terms of national security, cultural identity, or economic impact. From the standpoint of national security, for example, the primary concern is to control the border. Those trying to enter the country in any manner not permitted by law are categorized logically, then, as intruders and must be kept out. In contrast, a human rights perspective has as its special focus the needs and fate of the immigrants themselves. Immigration has been treated as a human rights issue within legal theory and international law for some time.[5]

Human rights language, however, raises red flags for some people. On occasion it has been used arbitrarily by a few special interest groups, and this makes many suspicious of any reference to human rights. Whatever may be the ideological basis of those organizations, however, the point here is a biblical one. Immigrants are made in the image of God. Believers must examine their hearts for possible contrary allegiances that might lead them to want to deny entry to those from elsewhere—whether this be on cultural, racial, socioeconomic, educational, or political grounds. Misconceptions also arise from the tendency to generalize. Some assume that all Hispanics are the same, when in fact they come from different countries, each with its own history, customs, food, and religious traditions; nor do all Hispanics come from the same racial, social, economic, or educational backgrounds. The image of God should lead to an appreciation of the worth and potential of Hispanics, both as a group and as individuals.

At the same time, of course, each person of the majority culture is made in the image of God, too. This fact can add an interesting element to attitudes toward those from other countries. In the Old Testament God is portrayed as limitlessly compassionate not only toward his own people (Exod. 34:6–7; Joel 2:13) but also to those beyond the community of faith. In the book of Jonah, the prophet admits that the God of Israel would be merciful even to the Assyrians, the cruelest empire of that time (Jon. 4:2; cf. Ps. 145:8–9). His grace knows no bounds. One way those of the majority culture can reflect the divine image is to demonstrate that same compassion to others—in this case, to immigrants, who have come to seek a better life in this country.

It must be made clear at this juncture that this conviction in no way implies that there should be no control over immigration or no order at the country's southern border. What the image-of-God premise does, though, is establish a basic mind-set from which one can begin to formulate policy and evaluate pragmatic decisions that must be made in the many spheres of national life. It should inform the tone of Christian participation in the national debate.

Expectations of the image. This word about the image of God has important things to convey to immigrant believers, too. First of all, it can be an encouragement. For many reasons, immigrants can feel inferior and of less worth. They may have less schooling, come from a more deprived economic background, and have a hard time learning English or speak what they do know with an accent. They may not know the laws or handle cultural cues well; many live in perpetual fear of the authorities. The fact that they are made in God's image should generate a more edifying perspective about themselves—about who they are and what they can become, about what they can add to their new context and to the common good. Whatever their previous or present condition, they are valuable before God and, therefore, to the United States.

Not surprisingly, this theme of the image of God and Hispanic identity and worth is a major topic in Hispanic theological writing. What these authors try to convey is that Hispanics have significance not only as humans in a general sense but, just as important, also *as Hispanic persons*. It is at this point that the theme of *mestizaje*, which was mentioned in the previous chapter, comes into play theologically and pastorally.[6] Ethnicity is no longer something to be ashamed of. *Mestizaje* can be embraced as a gift from God and is inseparable from being a valued human—a unique person, one from a special people with a matchless history and culture. Immigrants have an intrinsic dignity as humans and as Hispanics.

The image of God makes a claim on Hispanics as well. The fact that immigrants are made in God's image should cause them to reflect on what his expectations of them might be. Their divine endowment has profound implications for the way they develop their capabilities in education and at the workplace; it should impact how immigrants carry out their responsibilities as potential citizens, raise their families, work at their jobs, handle their money, and generally engage the world in which they now live.[7] In addition, immigrants should value the people of this country as those made in God's image. To be too easily critical of things Anglo or African-American as a defensive reaction to prejudice or in order to extol the mores of Latin American cultures at the expense of others is to contradict what Hispanics themselves seek: appreciation for their abilities and for their different backgrounds. For the Hispanic, as for the majority culture, being God's representative is both a *privilege* and a *responsibility*.

Through its instruction on the image of God, the Bible can mold the attitudes and actions of the majority culture and Hispanic Christians. For the former, it can yield fresh appreciation of the immigrants' value and promise; for the latter, its message is one of encouragement to forge ahead and an exhortation to live well as God's representatives.

The Experiences of the People of God

A second way in which the Old Testament can inform immigration discussions is through its accounts of the many people of God who moved across borders. This movement involved individuals, families, or large groups. Sometimes it was voluntary. In other instances it was forced.

Some might contend that the Bible does not present details of the lives of immigrants but rather of refugees. Therefore, it would not be appropriate to appeal to the Scriptures for a study on immigration per se. This observation is true in a strictly technical sense with respect to some biblical passages. Nevertheless, it ignores the fact that not all the migrations recorded in the Old Testament were of refugees. This argument overlooks the fact that immigration is not only about the reasons and mechanics of the move *to* another place; it is about life *in* that new setting. In this regard, there are lessons to be gleaned from the Old Testament irrespective of *how* these persons found themselves out of their land.

> ... immigration is not only about the reasons and mechanics of the move *to* another place; it is about life *in* that new setting.

Others might object to the following survey by pointing out that the accounts of the Hebrew Bible describe the experiences of Israel (and Judah), not of any and all immigrants. The question that could be posed to me is whether I am seeking to equate all Hispanic immigrants with God's people. The answer is "no"—even though, of course, there is a large multitude of believers among those who come.

The purpose of presenting this material is twofold. First, these biblical passages demonstrate how central migrations are to much of the Hebrew Bible. This awareness should alert us to how universal this phenomenon is, and it can impact our understanding of what these texts portray and teach us. Second, these accounts depict how migrant people responded to circumstances in their day. These responses are quite similar to what Hispanic (and all) immigrants go through. The text, in other words, can make readers more sensitive to the immigrant population and the challenges they face.

In the end, these contentions, although trying to be faithful to the biblical text, miss the important truth of God's concern for the vulnerable. His is a deep love for the needy and disenfranchised, whoever they are and whatever the cause of their situation. His is not selective mercy. He cares for each human, because each one, as we have seen, is made in his image. The most fundamental tenet of the Christian faith is that God loved the entire world so much that he sent his son Jesus to die for all humanity (John 3:16). The Bible also teaches that he is sovereignly involved in the movements of all peoples (Amos 9:7). Today, this would mean that he is present in some way in the migrations we are witnessing worldwide.

What follows is organized under three general headings. Classifying the biblical accounts in this way can lead to a better appreciation of the various reasons people in the Old Testament migrated and how they responded in each situation.

Hunger

The patriarchs. The book of Genesis recounts the stories of several migrations. Abram (he will not be called Abraham until Gen. 17:5) and his extended family leave Ur of the Chaldeans at God's command and move to Canaan (Gen.

11:31–12:9). This relocation, however, did not signify that they settled permanently in one place. The patriarch and his descendents lived a nomadic life, even in the promised land. The only piece of land Abraham is said to have owned was the cave of Machpelah, which he bought from Ephron the Hittite in order to have a plot in which to bury his wife Sarah (Gen. 23; cf. 49:29–33). In numerous places in Genesis the patriarchs are called "sojourners" or they are said to "sojourn" in an area for a time: Abraham (17:8; 20:1; 21:34; 23:4), Isaac (35:27; 37:1), Jacob (28:4; 32:4 [32:5 MT]), and Jacob's sons (47:4, 9).[8] In fact, this itinerant experience so marked Israel's identity that years later it became a part of the confession spoken by the head of the household when presenting the firstfruits of the harvest to the LORD (Deut. 26:5; cf. 1 Chron. 29:15; Ps. 39:12 [39:13 MT]).

Not too long after arriving in Canaan, Abram journeys to Egypt (Gen. 12:10). There is a famine in the land promised by God, and he and his family seek food. The climatic conditions in that part of the world are precarious, and nomads can be particularly at risk. The patriarch abandons Canaan and looks for sustenance in Egypt. Because of the massive Nile River and the rich soil in the delta and along its banks, Egypt was considered the breadbasket of the region. Egyptians were accustomed to receiving immigrants, whether for short-term or long-term stays, although reaction to them varied. A series of defense systems were established to keep some out, but small bands continually made their way to Egypt.[9] Out of fear Abram presents Sarah as his sister (12:10–20). He would repeat this cowardly act when he comes to the territory of Abimelech, the king of the Philistines (Gen. 20).

Isaac would also move to Philistine territory because of a famine (26:1). Jacob sends his sons twice to Egypt to buy food as the shortages worsened (41:57–42:6; 43:1–7). Eventually he and his sons and their families move to Egypt. There under Joseph's provision they are able to escape the hunger (47:10–13). In each of these cases, the one receiving the migrant patriarch and his family is charitable and willing to meet their needs.

Ruth. Another instance of a family moving to another country in time of famine occurred during the period of the Judges and is found in the book of Ruth. In order to survive, Elimelech, his wife Naomi, and their two sons leave their farm in Bethlehem. They cross the Jordan to dwell in the plains of Moab, and there the sons marry Moabite women (Ruth 1:1–2). Within a span of just a few verses, the narrative provides a second example of immigration, literally in the opposite direction. Apparently Elimelech dies soon after the arrival in Moab, and within ten years his sons die, too (vv. 3–5). The three widows are left to provide for themselves. Naomi and one of her daughters-in-law, Ruth, decide to go back to Bethlehem, because they had heard that the LORD was providing food for his people there (vv. 6–19).

These two solitary women—one an Israelite, the other a foreign dependent, related by marriage—do return, but they struggle to make ends meet. Their situations are now reversed: Naomi the immigrant has come home; Ruth, who had married a foreigner, has become the immigrant in a strange land. The younger woman goes to the fields every day to gather food to support her Israelite mother-in-law and herself. Eventually her hard work and stellar character incur the favor of Naomi's kinsman Boaz. He redeems Naomi's property and, in accordance with levirate law, marries Ruth. Through Boaz's marriage to this Moabite and the son born of that relationship, the ancestral land is able to remain within the family (Ruth 4:1–17a; cf. Deut. 25:5–9). Boaz fulfills his familial obligation, but he does not do this grudgingly. He is gracious to this immigrant woman in need, even though she is a Moabite, to whom the law was less than favorable (Num. 22–25; Deut. 23:3).

The final verses of the book reveal that this tale of loyalty and generosity is an important thread in the much larger tapestry of the lineage of David (Ruth 4:17b–22). Who at that time could have guessed that this Moabite immigrant would affect the history of the nation's monarchy and centuries later represent a stage in the genealogy of the Messiah (Matt. 1:5)! The day-to-day activities and decisions of these individuals were all pieces of the broader jigsaw puzzle of history. The lives of Ruth the immigrant and those around her would echo for centuries and play a key role in the unfolding of the plan of God.

At the same time, Ruth assimilates to some degree into Israelite culture. She must have learned Hebrew to be able to communicate with her husband's family and later with the people of his home village, Bethlehem. Ruth abandons her people to join Naomi's people and forsakes her gods to embrace the god of Naomi, Yahweh (the LORD) the God of Israel (Ruth 1:16–17). In doing so, Ruth echoes the covenant formula between the LORD and Israel: "I will take you as my own people, and I will be your God" (Exod. 6:7; cf. Lev. 26:12). In the ancient world, to leave one's gods was to renounce a crucial element of national and cultural identity. To believe in the deity of another people, and all that would entail, meant to enter into the very core of their existence and adopt their worldview. Ruth also follows the levirate marriage arrangement (Ruth 4:9–13) together with its implications for inheritance, which were connected to the promises of God to his people (Deut. 25:5–10).

In other words, this law was full of theological and cultural significance. This marriage signified yet another step into the world of Ruth's adopted home. The book of Ruth, therefore, is not only a tale of this woman's praiseworthy responses to Naomi and Boaz; it is also a testimony to her admirable attitudes *as an immigrant.*

Forced Exile

Joseph. In addition to cases of migration to other places in search of food and water, there are instances where individuals or groups are forced to leave the land against their will. In the book of Genesis, Joseph is sold by his brothers to passing Midianite traders. These in turn take him to Egypt and sell him to Potiphar, an officer of Pharaoh (Gen. 37:28, 36). This unfortunate immigrant, in a place not of his own choosing and far from his family, proved to be a faithful worker with high moral standards. But Joseph's uprightness seems to no avail, as he is wrongly accused of molesting his master's wife and put in prison (Gen. 39). In jail Joseph confirms his integrity and wisdom, and eventually he is promoted to be governor over Egypt, one of the most powerful nations in the world (chaps. 40–41). This immigrant ends up saving the nation from famine.

Joseph accommodates himself to Egyptian life in a variety of ways. When he is to be brought before Pharaoh, he is shaved according to Egyptian custom (41:14). The ceremonial promotion of Joseph also fits that context (41:41–43). He is given an Egyptian name and marries an Egyptian woman, with whom he has two sons; the names of his sons indicate, though, that he has forgotten neither his god nor his home (41:45, 50–52). The longing to return to his land is repeated just before his death (50:24–25; cf. Exod. 13:19; Josh. 24:32). Joseph adopts the dress and make-up commensurate with his social station to such an extent that his brothers do not recognize him (Gen. 43:8; 45:1–15). Joseph observes another cultural convention when he serves them food: it was not permitted for Egyptians to eat with the Hebrews, and so his family is served separately (43:32). When Joseph dies, he is embalmed and placed in a coffin, according to Egyptian practice (50:26), as he had done with his father, Jacob (50:3).

The respect and affection Joseph earned from the Egyptians is made manifest when they share his grief at Jacob's death (50:4–14). From archaeological reliefs and inscriptions we learn that Egypt assimilated many foreigners into their economic, social, military, and political spheres.[10] Joseph is an illustration of this openness, and he follows the cultural accommodations that are found elsewhere in this material.

Daniel. Joseph is not the only person deported from his homeland who served in a high position in the government of another country. Another example is Daniel. He was taken from Jerusalem along with other promising young men by the Babylonian king Nebuchadnezzar (Dan. 1:1–4a). Babylonian foreign policy entailed taking the best of the leadership from conquered territories and retraining them for posts within the imperial bureaucracy. During his time in Babylon, Daniel served four kings of two empires (Dan. 1–6): the Babylonians Nebuchadnezzar and Belshazzar, and the Persians Darius and Cyrus. Throughout his long tenure this immigrant statesman steadfastly maintained his faith in the LORD and on several occasions was willing to sacrifice his life rather than compromise his beliefs. His uprightness was applauded by several of these kings.

From the very beginning Daniel has to determine the appropriate level of accommodation to Babylonian culture, not only in a general sense but also within the charged political atmosphere of the national palace. The program to which he and his friends are assigned was designed to prepare them to better serve the empire. It involved teaching them a new language, re-educating them in the literature and ways of Babylon, providing them a different diet, and giving them Babylonian names—all important components of cultural identity (1:4b–7). Commentaries often remark that Daniel and three others refused to compromise on the food because of the strictures of Jewish dietary law and that this refusal demonstrates the strength of their faith. This is true theologically, but what is missed is the very thing cultural studies would underscore: food is central to how a people lives out who they are. One has only to look at the ethnic restaurants and grocery stores in immigrant communities or how American tourists look for McDonald's to recognize how integral food is to self-definition. To maintain a separate diet in Daniel's case would be pleasing to the LORD because of its religious meaning, yes, but it would also be a tangible way for him and his keepers to recognize his particular cultural boundaries (1:8–16). Another cultural marker was his prayer life, which in time got him into trouble and thrown into the lion's den (6:5–16).

Deportees. The biblical text also mentions the removal or the flight of many others, but oftentimes these people are not named in the biblical accounts. They are the masses who are the helpless victims of the cruelties of war and the material want that comes in its aftermath. When Samaria, the capital of the Northern Kingdom, was sacked by the Assyrians in 722 BC (and attacked a second time in 720 BC), thousands were forcibly carried off to different parts of the empire (2 Kings 17:1–6, 23; 18:9–11). Archaeological finds reveal a sudden surge in the population of the Southern Kingdom of Judah in the last quarter of the eighth century BC, surely the result of a major flow southward of refugees fleeing the Assyrian onslaught.[11] Just a few years later (701 BC), another Assyrian king, Sennacherib, laid siege to Jerusalem. Even though unable to subjugate the city, in his annals Sennacherib claims to have taken away a huge number of prisoners and booty from his war against Judah.[12] When the city was put under siege for the first time by King Nebuchadnezzar of Babylon in 597 BC, ten thousand were deported (2 Kings 24:14–16). Jerusalem finally fell a decade later (587/586 BC). What remained of

> . . . food is central to how a people lives out who they are.

the elite and a few thousand others were sent away (2 Kings 25:7, 11, 21; 2 Chron. 36:18, 20; Jer. 52:27–31).

Escapees. There are examples, too, of individuals who flee to another country in order to save their lives. Several are prominent figures in biblical history. Moses escaped from Egypt after killing a taskmaster (Exod. 2:11–14). He settled in Midian for forty years, and there he married a woman, Zipporah (2:15–22). They had a son, whom Moses named Gershom, saying "I have become a sojourner in a foreign land" (2:22). The boy's name is a word play on the Hebrew *gēr* ("sojourner"), a key term that will be examined in the next chapter. Of course, Moses, an Israelite, had grown up in Pharaoh's court. His name is probably of Egyptian origin (although this is a point of contention among some scholars), and Moses was given an education worthy of his social standing (2:5–10; cf. Heb. 11:23–27). The skills in leadership and the military arts learned in the royal palace would prepare him for the role he would later have in leading the Israelites out of Egypt.[13] The training of this foreigner, in other words, was an important part of God's plan to free his people. Ironically, his assimilation process in due course moves in a reverse direction—from the adopted Egyptian context to his Israelite roots. Moses needed both cultures (including their languages) to engage Pharaoh and his court and to fulfill his divine calling to guide his people to the promised land.

Similarly, David had to run from Saul and live among the Philistines (1 Sam. 27). Jeroboam went down to Egypt to get away from Solomon, who sought to kill him after Jeroboam received the prophetic word from Ahijah that he would be king over ten of Israel's tribes (1 Kings 11:29–40; 12:2–3). Jeremiah and his scribe Baruch were taken to Egypt by those who had been involved in the assassination of the Babylonian governor Gedaliah. Gedaliah had been appointed by the king of Babylon to rule over the region after the fall of Jerusalem. The conspirators and their followers feared the vengeance of the empire, and even though the prophet told them that they should trust the LORD and stay, they fled to Egypt and took him with them (Jer. 40–44).

Life as Foreigners

The Old Testament not only provides accounts of the plight of those taken to other countries and of those who had been forced to flee; it also describes the life of their descendents in those faraway lands. There are two central historical experiences of the people of God staying in other places for long periods: the sojourn in Egypt and the exile in Assyria and Babylon.

Egypt. The beginning of the account in the book of Exodus is far removed from the days of Joseph. Other passages inform us that the Israelites' stay in Egypt lasted about four hundred years (Gen. 15:13; cf. Acts 7:6). For an undisclosed time the Israelites experienced protection under Joseph and those who had known him, but now they had been reduced to slavery. As slaves, they worked on royal building projects and in agriculture (Exod. 1:11–14).

Even as they benefited from the Israelites' toil, Pharaoh and the Egyptians feared the surprising increase in the number of the Israelites (1:9–13, 20; 5:5). They were willing to take advantage of the cheap labor of this foreign people as long as they were "invisible." Once the population of Israelites increased and their presence no longer was as unexceptional, however, the Egyptians began to worry. They took measures to control this growth, to the point of decreeing state-sponsored infanticide (1:15–2:4), but there never was any question of curtailing their labor or alleviating their work. The response to complaints and insubordination was to prescribe higher and more difficult quotas (5:6–21). The empire needed these foreigners to complete their construction projects and to work the fields to feed its populace. Life for the Isrealites was hard and their overlords cruel. This description agrees with extra-biblical evidence of Semites serving as slaves in ancient Egypt.[14]

In the midst of their suffering the Israelites cry out to God, and God answers (2:23–25). The structure of the narrative in Exodus is instructive. Before the lament of the people is recorded, Moses is placed in Midian (2:15–22), where he would receive the revelation at the burning bush (3:1–10). The plan of God, in other words, had already been set in motion. Under Moses they would go to Canaan, where they could live as a free people in a new place that offered them a better quality of existence, a "land flowing with milk and honey" (3:5, 17). There they would have their own homes and vineyards, a blessing denied them as slaves (Deut. 6:11; Josh. 24:13). The rest of the Pentateuch is the story of how they reached the border of that promised land.

Assyria and Babylon. The second setting for life in another region described in some detail in the Old Testament is the exile in Babylon after the defeat of Judah. While some had been carried away before that time (such as Daniel and Ezekiel, among others), as was mentioned above, a final deportation took place after the destruction of Jerusalem. The Old Testament contains a lot of material that portrays the fate and feelings of the Judeans in Babylon. It is silent, however, about the Israelites who had been taken by the Assyrians from the Northern Kingdom in 722 and 720 BC and from Judah in 701 BC. In a fortuitous turn of events, archaeologists have discovered inscriptional data and reliefs that provide a good bit of information about the life of deportees in the Neo-Assyrian Empire.[15]

Administrative documents reveal that the fortunes of individuals and of families were quite varied. Much depended on the skills these persons might have and what the particular needs of the empire might be at the moment. Those who were carpenters or smiths fared fairly well, as did those who were put into government positions. Some troops and charioteers were absorbed into the imperial armies; other deportees apparently were merchants. The less fortunate were conscripted into service as domestics or were assigned to harsh labor on farms or on building projects. Some assimilation appears to have taken place, and one would expect that this process would have differed according to circumstances and social standing. That this occurred is evident by data suggesting that later generations took non-Israelite names. It also would have been necessary to acquire the language of their captives; intermarriage was inevitable.

The Old Testament portrayal of life in Babylon is extensive, covering the fate of the royal family to that of the more common people.[16] It was customary to have captured kings live in the palace. They were viewed as living trophies, and their treatment depended on the good graces of the victorious monarch. Jehoiachin, who was a victim of Nebuchadnezzar's siege of 597 BC, was taken along with his family and officials (2 Kings 24:10–16). The book of 2 Kings closes with a notice of his eventual promotion among the other defeated kings. The Babylonians considered him to be the last legitimate ruler of Judah (25:27–30). He was given a seat of honor at the table of Evil-merodach, Nebuchadnezzar's son, and provided new clothes and a stipend. Fate was not as kind to Zedekiah. After Jerusalem had been taken, his sons were killed and his eyes gouged out; he was then carried away in chains (25:6–7). He is not heard of again.

The text offers glimpses of the feelings of some of the recent arrivals in Babylon. Psalm 137 is a lament that expresses the pain over loss, above all over the ruin of Jerusalem—with its palace, the symbol of the Davidic dynasty and hope of glory, and the temple, the special place of God's dwelling and center of their faith. There is sorrow, shame, and anger; it is a veritable roller coaster of emotions about being so far from everything that gave meaning and order to life. Some exiles expected a quick return. Indeed, a few prophets were announcing as much (Jer. 28). But Jeremiah sends a letter to the exiles and tells them that their stay in Babylon will be a long one, at least seventy years (Jer. 29). The letter is interesting because it counsels them to invest in their new land. They are to build houses, plant their gardens, marry and raise families, and pray for God's blessing on that place (Jer. 5–7). We do not know how many of those in Babylon received this communication.

Ezekiel lived and ministered among the exiles (Ezek. 1:1–2; 2:15), but he does not mention Jeremiah. The fact that there are elders still functioning within the community of exiles indicates that the people enjoyed some level of autonomy in terms of local life.

Return to the land. It is clear that the hope of a return to the promised land burned in the hearts of many of the Jews in exile. Testimony to this fact is the series of three returns from Babylon, first under Zerubbabel (Ezra 1–3), then under Ezra (Ezra 7–8), and last under Nehemiah (Neh. 2). This does not mean, however, that there had been no adjustments made to the majority culture in Babylon. Before he returns to Jerusalem, Nehemiah had risen to a place of prominence and unique trust as the king's cupbearer (Neh. 1:11). He must have assimilated the language, customs, and political protocols to have achieved that position. Still, he maintains a strong bond to the land of his fathers (1:1–4) and his faith in God (1:5–11; 2:4–5). Ezra, as a priest, naturally holds his cultural-religious boundaries more tightly and is recognized as a religious leader of another people by the Persian authorities (Ezra 7:1–12, 21, 25).

The cultural dynamic of the move back is complex.[17] The books of Ezra and Nehemiah demonstrate that it involved more than a geographical change. The return was part of a larger set of commitments, tightly bound to the ancient traditions. There was concern for legitimacy (hence, the genealogies), the reclaiming of the holy place and the reinstitution of proper ritual (the rebuilding of the altar and the temple, the celebration of Passover), and the fear of disobedience and uncleanness (the problem of mixed marriages). Lineage, religious life, and marital boundaries were all part of the Jewish cultural self-definition—and preservation. But what sustained them, too, was hope. Prophetic words had assured them that, even though they were a defeated people and an insignificant minority within an empire, the LORD their God was mightier than the deities of Babylon and any other political power (Isa. 40, 44–46; Dan. 2–7). Haggai and Zechariah had stood beside them as they built a new temple. These prophets and others in the past had foretold the coming of a king who would rule over a restored Israel and over all the nations in justice and peace (Isa. 9, 11, 32; Jer. 33; Ezek. 36–48; Hag. 2; Zech. 9). Things would be different from what they had been for so long.

Their identity as Jews would be experienced in a different way. Those who returned were not the same people. They had seen the world and the great cities of its most powerful empires. They had lived among another people and participated in different ways of life within a context so unlike their own. Going home was a return to the same place, but the returnees and even that place called "home" had changed. The opposition they endured, such as what Nehemiah faced from within and without the community, may have been due to the competing agendas and aspirations of those who did not want to see the status quo changed (Neh. 4–6).[18]

Persia. But not everyone went back to the land. Many stayed behind. The story of Esther is a case in point. There is no inkling that either she or her uncle Mordechai had given any thought of living anywhere else. There is the tension in the narrative of being part of the larger society, yet at the same time members of a marginalized community. Mordechai forbids Esther from revealing her

84

cultural background to King Ahasuerus (Esther 2:9–11, 20), and Haman desires to single out the Jews because of their difference—at least in the case of Mordechai, who refused to bow before him (3:1–6). Esther in the end does reveal her background (8:5–6) and saves her people from destruction (8:11–9:17). This event is the basis of the Jewish festival of Purim (9:18–32), which is celebrated to this day.

Cultural accommodation percolates under the surface. Even though Mordechai is a Jew of the tribe of Benjamin, his name is probably connected to Marduk, the chief god of Babylon. Recent discoveries demonstrate that it was a common name, so there probably is no religious significance attached to it. The point, however, is that it is not an Israelite name. Perhaps he had two names, the other a Hebrew one, as did his niece Esther (see below). Mordechai denounces a plot to kill the king (2:19–23). Was this out of loyalty and appreciation to the crown? Apparently, Mordechai was doing well financially, too. Several times the text says that he sits at the king's gate (2:19, 21; 3:2; 5:9, 13; 6:10, 12). This might be an indication of his stature, as normally only men of importance would sit there. This also would explain Haman's anger. If Mordechai were poor and unimportant, his lack of deference would not have been so insulting.

Esther has two names: the Hebrew name Hadassah, and the Babylonian or Persian name Esther (2:7). She goes willingly to the royal harem.[19] Esther also quickly learns the ways of the palace and how to manipulate the king by organizing fabulous feasts. Whatever faith the two of them may have had is only subtly communicated by Mordechai's famous line, "And who knows but that you have come to royal position for such a time as this" (4:14) and Esther's call for a fast (4:15–16; cf. 4:3).[20] The first hints at a trust in the sovereignty of the LORD; the second is common religious practice.

The number of those slain by the Jews would indicate that many thousands were in Susa, the capital city, and in the other provinces of the Persian empire (9:5–17). In fact, the Jewish community in that part of the world—now modern day Iraq—would flourish for centuries. One of its enduring contributions to Judaism is the Babylonian Talmud. Only a handful of Jews remain there today.[21]

Implications for Today

Realism and everyday life. The Old Testament is full of accounts of people on the move or who have settled in other places. Many reasons are given for this movement, and these migrations—whether of individuals or of large groups—span centuries. They are part of the fabric of biblical history—and ours. This realization offers a lesson to the majority culture. Migrations are a recurring phenomenon. Accordingly, Hispanic immigration to the United States is but another chapter in the very long book of the annals of humankind. That being the case, one can step back and try to appreciate why people, then and now, are compelled to go to another place.

The text gives a human face to the migrants. They are tested and discriminated against; they want to have a home and provide for their families; they worship God; they work at different jobs, some not by their own choice; others are gifted in special ways, rise to positions of authority, and do marvelous things for the country in which they live; some long to return to their homeland while others choose to stay in their new country; and they wrestle with how to coordinate their backgrounds with the different culture that surrounds them—the issues of language, customs, faith, politics, economics, and laws. These are also flawed individuals. They sin; they are imperfect in all kinds of ways.

In other words, the Bible offers the reader very realistic scenes and situations and amazingly true-to-life characters. These immigrants and refugees are *people* above all else, people caught up in the trials, tribulations, and joys of life. It is *everyday life*, but the text teaches that these lives are set against a much bigger canvas. These people are part of the plan of God for the unfolding of world history. Consequently, the majority culture must evaluate its reaction to immigrants. The Old Testament recounts the compassionate actions of some as well as the cruelty of others toward foreigners. Herein are examples, good and bad, to be followed and avoided.

A creative space. Another fascinating point to ponder is the wealth of biblical books of assorted genres that were produced by those living outside the promised land. Being away from the familiar proved to be a creative space for thinking about God, life, the direction of history, and the nature of hope. Perhaps there is a lesson in this. There is much we can learn about the Christian faith from immigrants, from those outsiders whose pilgrimage with God has been on another path.

Analogous situations. For today's immigrants, this Old Testament material can serve other ends. It has the potential to be a divine mirror, where they see themselves and identify with its descriptions and its characters. Immigrants can actually "live" the text's scenes, because they have gone through similar experiences and have dealt with comparable emotions, tensions, and challenges.

> These immigrants and refugees are *people* above all else, people caught up in the trials, tribulations, and joys of life.

Many immigrants seek a "promised land" of a better existence, a "land of milk and honey." But the trek here is hard, and life once they get to the United States can be full of long hours of work with low pay and few benefits. Perhaps they have left one Egypt for another. Here the majority culture fears their numbers and their being different, although they want their labor.

A number of Hispanic theologians emphasize the exile as the most appropriate paradigm for understanding the

Hispanic situation.[22] The United States is the place to which they literally have moved, and they sense the separation from their home country quite concretely. This is an exile not in the sense that they are here as refugees or deportees; it is an exile because conditions in their home country compelled them to leave. And so they arrive from Mexico, Puerto Rico, Cuba, Guatemala, El Salvador, and elsewhere in the Americas. But it is not the same for other Hispanics. In contrast to the recent arrivals, they have been here as long as they can remember, and millions are second- or third-generation descendants of immigrants. Theirs is not a physical exile but rather an interior one.

The backgrounds and experiences of Hispanics are infinitely diverse, but for all, life here is new, different, and difficult. Like the people of the Bible, they wrestle with language, other ways of doing things, an unknown political system and set of laws, and marginalization. What is "home"? Where is it? Who are we? What might it mean to "seek the peace of the city" (Jer. 29:7)[23] today and in this place? What are the appropriate parameters of accommodation or assimilation to this country? There is a wonderful title to a book in Spanish that captures this engagement between text and context so powerfully: *en la dispersión, el texto es patria* ("in the diaspora, the text is the home country").[24] The Bible, in other words, is where Hispanics can find themselves and God in their "exile."

But if what immigrants see in the text is themselves, then—if that seeking is honest—what they also see are sinners. It will not do to idealize their situation or culture; the Old Testament does not do this. Its realism reminds us that the movement of peoples is not tidy and that any group is a mixed lot.

In the Bible's richness, much is available for the majority culture and the immigrant. To the former it reveals that migration is a human condition to be appreciated and demands a response of grace. For those who are sojourners there is much to ponder there about life and faith. The text is a mirror in which is found similar experiences as well as a candid view of immigrant life.

Conclusion

This chapter has covered a lot of ground. It began with the theme of the image of God and what it means to be human. This must be the place where all Christians begin any discussion about immigration. The next major section rehearsed the many instances of migration in the Old Testament and pointed out their different causes. It also discussed the variety of cultural and faith responses of both migrants and host peoples.

The complicated picture in the text is very real. Today the situation is complicated, too! This is good news. The Bible is complex enough to connect with the realities of human life. If its depictions are so true to life, as the Word of God, it can also orient believers of the majority culture and the immigrant community as to the proper attitudes and perspectives with which both sides should engage the national debate.

The next chapter continues the exploration of the Old Testament. It will locate the treatment of the immigrant within the general ethos of hospitality that was common in the ancient world as it appears in the Bible. The second section will detail the legislation concerning foreigners in Israel's law. Attitudes are important, but sooner or later any society must regulate itself in concrete ways. It is no different in our world today.

3

THE LAW AND
THE SOJOURNER

Guidance from the Old Testament, Part II

Give me your tired, your poor,
Your huddled masses yearning to breathe free,
The wretched refuse of your teeming shore.
Send these, the homeless, tempest-tost, to me,
I lift my lamp beside the golden door!

These immortal words come from a poem written by
Emma Lazarus titled "The New Colossus." It was written in 1883 to help in the effort to raise money for
the construction of the pedestal for the Statue of Liberty
in New York harbor. The statue had been commissioned as
a French gift to commemorate the centennial of American
independence in 1876 but was not completed until 1886.

It was not until 1903, though, that Lazarus's poem was engraved on a plaque and placed inside the pedestal.

Over the years, and not infrequently in the current debate, these lines have been used to claim that the Statue of Liberty stands as a powerful symbol of the fact that the United States is a nation of immigrants. Some dispute this view.[1] I will not contest the repudiation of the immigrant interpretation; it is enough for me to emphasize that at the very least this 125-year-old memorial and this poem communicate a charitable openness, an ethos of national hospitality to the vulnerable.

This notion of generous hospitality toward others pervades the Old Testament. As the previous chapter emphasized, attitudes are fundamental to how one views and treats the stranger. This chapter opens with a brief exploration of the ethics of hospitality in ancient Israel. The second section surveys Old Testament laws concerning immigrants and other foreigners. In the end, attitudes toward immigrants must be made concrete and systematized in legislation that defines their obligations and rights and that regulates the actions of the majority culture toward them. It was no different in Israel. It is the same today.

Hospitality in the Ancient World

Old Testament Practices

Travel in Old Testament times could be treacherous. There were potential dangers to be faced on the road, and there was the problem of finding sufficient food and drink and a safe haven en route. The cultures of the ancient Near East responded to these needs with shared conventions of hospitality toward the stranger. There were protocols and expectations for the host to be openhanded and for visitors not to abuse their welcome. It was assumed, too, that this act of kindness would be reciprocated, if and when the host were to journey to the guest's land.

Israel was not an exception to this widespread cultural ethic.[2] Perhaps the most notable example of this practice in the Old Testament is Abraham's interaction with the three strangers who appear at his tent in Genesis 18. The patriarch comes out to greet them and immediately offers them the best refreshment he can before they continue on their way. Scenes of liberal hospitality also occur in Genesis 24, when Rebekah's brother Laban offers food to Abraham's servant and provision for his camels; in Exodus 2, where the Midianite Ruel chastises his daughters for not inviting the "Egyptian" Moses to have something to eat; in Judges 19, with the repeated invitation of the concubine's father for the Levite to stay with the family; and in 2 Kings 4, with the care given to Elisha by the Shunammite couple. How self-sacrificing this commitment to others could be is exemplified by the poor widow of Zarephath, who is willing to share what little she has for herself and her son with the prophet Elijah (1 Kings 17).

There are also cases where things go terribly wrong: Lot invites Abraham's guests, who have come to Sodom, into his home, but then is willing to sacrifice his daughters to protect the strangers (Gen. 19); in the second half of Judges 19 the Levite refuses to try the hospitality of Jebus (that is, Jerusalem), because it is not an Israelite city, and instead goes on to Gibeah, to horrific consequences.

> Hospitality to the stranger is a virtue

Hospitality to the stranger is a virtue. Job cites his care of the traveler as testimony to his integrity (Job 31:32), and in the book of Isaiah hospitality to the stranger is lifted up as proof of true faith in God (Isa. 58:6–7). Some even understand Psalm 23 to contain an allusion to the custom of hospitality (v. 5). If this interpretation is correct, then graciousness toward those in need is revealed to be an attribute of the LORD himself. It is no wonder, then, that this same charitable spirit and material sharing are expected to characterize the people of God. Whatever might have been the common cultural impulse to be hospitable to the stranger in ancient times is here given a more profound motivation. To be hospitable is to imitate God.

Implications for Today

The host. In the United States it seems as if it is becoming more and more difficult to be hospitable, to take the time to be with others and welcome them into one's home. Life is so busy and so full of activity, and families can be so fractured, that few are able to slow down and open their heart and hearth to anyone, let alone someone different. To cling to a chosen lifestyle and schedule, define the permitted parameters of a neighborhood, and monopolize time just for oneself and one's family to the exclusion of the stranger—any stranger—might be rebellion against God and an ignoring of something dear to him. The biblical challenge to be hospitable to the stranger is set before the individual Christian and Christian communities, whether large or small.

The theme of hospitality is relevant to the immigration debate. The biblical text can gently prod believers of the majority culture to a greater mind-set of hospitality and to actions of hospitality toward the strangers who are Hispanic immigrants. To be sure, there are other strangers among the normal day-to-day contacts of the majority culture. These could be the visitor at church, a neighbor, or someone at work. But there is an immense group of other strangers who cannot be ignored. What I am not doing here (and what I cannot do) is defining what shape that hospitality should take. It can take an infinite number of forms, from small gestures of greeting to broader scale concrete action through a ministry or organization directed toward the needs of immigrants. The key is having

94

an attitude of hospitality, a gracious spirit, toward these strangers. Might not majority culture Christians set an example in this for the rest of the nation?

The recipient. The call to hospitality cannot be limited to the majority culture. Biblically, there is the expectation that the sojourner will not abuse the hospitality that is extended. Sadly, there have been cases of immigrants who have taken advantage of the national social system and of well-meaning individuals for personal gain. There is also a criminal element within the Hispanic community (as there is in any community). These constitute a very small percentage within the immigrant population, but these are the ones at whom those who oppose immigration point, and they are the ones who appear on the nightly news. In this country, where a good portion of the majority culture is nervous and skeptical, this negative face of the Hispanic immigrant must be acknowledged. At the same time, and most important, the appreciation of the greater part of immigrants toward the United States needs to be communicated to the majority culture. I have been in prayer meetings with Hispanic pastors and Christians where, as a people of God, we have lifted up prayers of thanksgiving for the United States and for the opportunities it has afforded immigrants. This is the proper response of the beneficiary of hospitality, and it is pervasive among Hispanic believers.

If hospitality is important in the Old Testament, it is fundamental to the message of the New Testament as well. We will return to this theme and its possible lessons for today in the next chapter.

Legislation concerning the Sojourner

Hospitality functions primarily at the personal and familial level and on an informal basis. Its practice could suggest that a people have an openhandedness about them. A test of this possibility is to examine their laws and the structures of their society to ascertain whether the moral qualities of welcome and kindness toward the outsider find formal expression. Do they impact how the society actually operates?

Law in the Old Testament

Misunderstandings. Many Christians have a distorted view of Old Testament law. Based on a certain reading of some verses in the Pauline epistles, they hold to two erroneous presuppositions. First, for many, the Old Testament law equals sacrifices for sin, nothing more. This is wrong on several counts. To begin with, there are sacrifices that have nothing to do with forgiveness of sin (such as the grain and fellowship offerings in Lev. 2–3; 6:14–23; 7:11–26). In addition, and I will discuss this a bit later, the law touches many areas of life beyond the rituals of ancient Israel.

The second misunderstanding is that Jews since the time of Moses (and especially in Jesus's day) believed that they had to obey the law in order to earn the right to be the people of God. The thought is that theirs was a religion only of works, while, by contrast, Christians are freed from the unforgiving demands of the law and can proclaim that salvation is by God's grace through faith alone.

I do not disagree with the good news of the gospel, but this perspective reveals a flawed notion of what the Old Testament law is and how it works. For a more correct appreciation, it is helpful to look at the narrative where the law is given to Israel. The flow of that account makes it unmistakably plain that the law was not intended to provide a way for the nation to gain a relationship with God.

Narrative context of the law. In Exodus 19 the people of God have come under the guidance of Moses to a mountain in the desert of Sinai. There they will receive this unique revelation from the LORD. Note when this happens. Israel had already celebrated the Passover in Egypt, in which their first-born had been spared divine judgment by the blood of the lamb they sprinkled on the doorposts of their homes (Exod. 12). Then, the people miraculously crossed the Red/Reed Sea and witnessed the defeat of Pharaoh's army in its churning waters (13:17–14:31). In other words, when the law is given to the nation through Moses, it is directed at a redeemed people. It was not designed to show them *how to achieve redemption*; rather, its purpose was to show them *how to live as a redeemed people*. The account begins with "You yourselves have seen what I did to Egypt, and how I carried you on eagles' wings and brought you to myself" (19:4). The prologue to the Ten Commandments underscores the fact of their redemption: "I am the LORD your God, who brought you out of Egypt, out of the land of slavery" (20:2). The laws then follow this assertion.

The narrative context for the giving of the law can be expanded beyond the preceding chapters in the book of Exodus. In the call of Abram in Genesis 12, the patriarch is told that he and his descendents will be the channel of God's blessing to the rest of the world (vv. 1–3). Centuries later, when the law is entrusted to Israel, it is presented in such a way so as to communicate that the law itself and the society that it was to shape and regulate are to be a divine blessing. The key text is worth citing in full. Moses is speaking:

> See, I have taught you decrees and laws as the LORD my God commanded me, so that you may follow them in the land you are entering to take possession of it. Observe them carefully, for this will show your wisdom and understanding to the nations, who will hear about all these decrees and say, "Surely this great nation is a wise and understanding people." What other nation is so great as to have their gods near them the way the LORD our God is near us whenever we pray to him? And what other nation is so great as to have such righteous decrees and laws as this body of laws I am setting before you today? (Deut. 4:5–8)

The law and the nations. The content of the law and Israel's adherence to its statutes were designed to point the surrounding peoples to the greatness of God and his wisdom. But there is something more here. Christopher Wright uses the term "paradigm" to explain this other purpose of the law. He explains that these laws "constituted a concrete model, a practical, culturally specific, experimental exemplar of the beliefs and values they embodied."[3] Through the medium of the law and its incarnation in the nation, the moral demands of God would be visible in concrete ways. The law was to offer to the world of that time an example of what a life pleasing to God would look like. One stipulation of the law prescribed to Israel is the attitude toward and treatment of the stranger.

> Israel's stance toward the foreigner was part of the larger fabric of its ethical life. It was part of the ethos of what it meant to be the people of God.

The fact that this law was to be a light to the nations does not mean, however, that it would be unique, totally distinct from other ancient Near Eastern law codes. In fact, one should expect some degree of overlap between the laws of the Old Testament and the law collections of other cultures in that geographical area. For one thing, they all deal with conventional social issues, such as marriage, property rights and procedures for inheritance, loans, theft, and murder. Second, it is natural that the broadly shared cultural and historical milieu of Mesopotamia and Syro-Palestine yielded some commonalities in the language and content of these law codes.[4]

At the same time, there are important differences between Israelite law and these other collections. These differences are grounded ultimately in the character of the divine Lawgiver and in what he had done for his people. Recent studies demonstrate the dissimilarities, based on these two foundations, in such areas as the mercy shown to the poor and the political ideology of the monarchy.[5] This will also be apparent in our study of the treatment of the stranger.

One final pertinent observation remains to be made, and it comes from a discipline called interpretive anthropology.[6] Interpretive anthropology teaches us that—although most people do not perceive it in this way—a system of law generates and is a reflection of its culture. In other words, what a particular culture defines as "true" and "right" in terms of legal principles and process is actually its own sociohistorical construct. It has a history; there are reasons why things are the way they are and function as they do. A society's law attempts to put all of life in its proper place and organize its chaos and adjudicate its conflicts. It is, therefore, a window into that society's soul. How the law is structured, the kinds of privileges and protections it offers, the demands and limits it imposes, and the institutions it establishes reveal that society's system of values and priorities. It discloses what that society understands to be correct and good.

This perspective adds another dimension to what we have been saying about Old Testament law. We should recognize that the way it deals with the foreigner says something very important about the heart of Israel and of its God who gave them these rules. Wright is correct that the law was to be a paradigm for the world. Interpretive anthropology would add the insight that it is not just that specific laws serve as a model for other nations. The laws reflect something deeper: Israel's stance toward the foreigner was part of the larger fabric of its ethical life. It was part of the ethos of what it meant to be the people of God.

Terminology for the Sojourner

Four terms are used in the Old Testament to refer to outsiders. They are the nouns *gēr* and *tôšab*, and the adjectives *nokrî* and *zār*.[7] The English versions are irregular in their translations of these terms. Sometimes the same English word is used for several of them and different English words for the same Hebrew term. Accordingly, in what follows I will stay primarily with the transliteration of the Hebrew. The next few paragraphs are a bit technical, but these details can be helpful for our purposes.

Nokrî and zār. The last two words of the four, *nokrî* and *zār*, usually convey that something or someone is non-Israelite.[8] Sometimes this is a neutral, matter-of-fact usage. For instance, when Ruth first speaks to Boaz, she calls herself a foreigner (*nokriyyâ*; Ruth 2:10); she is, of course, a Moabite. Solomon uses the term to refer to those from other countries who would come to worship the LORD at the temple in Jerusalem (1 Kings 8:41, 43). Often, however, the idea of foreignness in both these terms carries a negative connotation. They are used to refer to enemies, strange gods, a licentious woman, or foreign women of another faith who could corrupt an Israelite.[9] In these cases, that which is foreign is perceived as bad or threatening.

On other occasions, *nokrî* (and perhaps *zār*)[10] can refer to foreigners who now dwell in Israel. The profile of the *nokrî* is not altogether clear. The little textual evidence we have suggests at least two nuances. To begin with, there is the impression that at least some of these people have not been in the land very long. David calls his loyal commander Ittai, a mercenary Gittite, a *nokrî* and then says, "You came only yesterday" (2 Sam. 15:19). Of course, this phrase is hyperbole, but it does imply that Ittai has only just arrived. This might partly explain Ruth's comment to Boaz, too; she had not been in Bethlehem very long. In neither case is this viewed as a negative characteristic.

In other instances, it appears that these outsiders have not integrated themselves fully into Israelite life. The law prohibits this kind of foreigner from becoming king (Deut. 17:15) and from participating in some of Israel's rituals (Exod. 12:43; Ezek. 44:7, 9; cf. Lev. 22:25). It seems that an aspect of their "strangeness" within Israel is that these immigrants may have maintained their own faith (Isa. 2:6; yet, 1 Kings 8:41, 43). In Israel, where religion was

100

basic to all of life, this refusal to believe in the LORD was frowned on.

Tôšab. The term *tôšab* is even more difficult to define. It occurs but a few times in the Old Testament. It is almost always found in parallel, either with the nouns "hireling" (Exod. 12:45; Lev. 22:10; 25:6, 40) or "sojourner" (*gēr*; Lev. 25:23, 35, 47; Num. 35:15).[11] That these persons can be hired hands and that they are listed with the sojourner suggests a couple of things. First, these foreigners (or at least some of them) were economically dependent. There were reasons for this, and we will return to this socioeconomic reality below. Second, there must have been some distinction between the *tôšab* and the sojourner for them to be mentioned together sometimes. They appear with the *nokrî* in the prohibition about the Passover (Exod. 12:43, 45), so maybe they, too, are not as fully assimilated as the *gēr*. We cannot be certain. The scarcity of verses does not allow any firm conclusions to be drawn.

Gēr. The term that is most pertinent to this study is *gēr*.[12] It appears especially in the legal material of the Pentateuch, and the next section will explore what those books have to say about these persons. This word has been translated into English as "alien," "resident alien," "stranger," or "sojourner." I will use the last of these in what follows.

Before I move on, though, at least one significant conclusion can be drawn from what has been said thus far. Israel had a long history of having other peoples dwelling in their midst; indeed, they had left Egypt as a "mixed multitude" (Exod. 12:38, 43–50; my translation). On the basis of this experience and revelation from God, Israel had formulated distinctions between foreigners and made value judgments about them. The variety in the terminology reflects this.[13] Sadly, the picture offered by word studies is not altogether clear, so tidy definitions are simply not possible.

We probably cannot say much more than distinctions were made based on Israel's interaction with these foreigners. But this is an important point. It is a natural consequence of having others live among a people. Difference is there for all to see. Yet in Israel difference did not remain at the level of observation or lead to sharp separation from all immigrants and others who had found their way to the land. What will prove to be impressive is to see how God calls his people to respond to the *gēr*.

Laws Pertaining to the Sojourner

Ancient Near Eastern law. The first thing that stands out in the study of the sojourner (*gēr*) in Old Testament law is the huge contrast that can be drawn with the other law codes of the ancient Near East. In the last chapter it was mentioned that there is evidence from administrative documents about the life of deportees in Assyria, Babylon, and Persia. Nevertheless, the law codes are almost totally silent about these people and about those who emigrate from these nations.[14] There are a very few laws that deal with the marital and property rights of someone who leaves for a time and returns (Laws of Eshnunna, law 30; Laws of Hammurabi, laws 30, 31, 136).[15] Law 41 of the Laws of Eshnunna refers to a foreigner who it seems is a merchant of some kind, but its interpretation is disputed. Whatever its correct meaning, however, notice the utter lack of references to the foreigner who had come to live there, no matter the reason and the circumstances. The legislation in the Old Testament could not be more different.[16] The laws are numerous, and they are gracious to the sojourner.

Life as a sojourner. The economy of Israel was agrarian. In the austere environment of that part of the world, life in rural areas could be difficult. The support of kinship groups was indispensable in times of drought, crop failures, disease, and death. Ownership of land was fundamental for making a living and supporting a family. Inheritance of property went along kinship lines, passing from the father to the appropriate male heir. The challenge that sojourners—those immigrants or refugees who had moved to Israel—faced when arriving in the land was that they had left behind their kinship network. As a result, they were without the help that only an extended family could offer. As foreigners, they were also excluded from the land tenure system. Sojourners, therefore, could be particularly vulnerable to the unexpected and sometimes harsh vicissitudes of life.

Without land and kin, many sojourners would be dependent on the Israelites for work, provision, and protection. They could be day laborers (Deut. 24:14), and the Old Testament mentions that they were conscripted to do the hard labor in the building of the temple (1 Chron. 22:2; 2 Chron. 2:17–18). Apparently, a few became successful, but these seem to be the exception to the rule (Lev. 25:47).

The law recognizes their potentially precarious situation and responds by including them with others who, too, would have been at risk: widows and orphans, other hired workers, servants, and the poor.[17] Along with these other unfortunates, sojourners qualified for the gleaning law. This stipulated that harvesters leave untouched the edges of a field so that the needy could gather food (Lev. 19:10; 23:22; Deut. 24:19–22). It is noteworthy that it is while Ruth is working among the harvesters that Boaz spots her (Ruth 2). Sojourners were also to receive a portion of the special tithe that was collected every three years for the poor (Deut. 14:28–29; 26:12–13). They were to be paid in a timely manner (Deut. 24:15) and allowed to rest on the Sabbath (Exod. 20:10; 23:12; Deut. 5:14). They were to receive fair treatment in legal cases; no prejudice against the foreigner was to be tolerated (Deut. 1:16–17) nor any advantage taken because they were powerless (Deut. 24:17–18; 27:19).

The prophets thundered against those Israelites who did not accept the responsibility to care for these folk. It was a breach of their faith in the LORD, and he would not tolerate this disobedience (Jer. 22:3; Ezek. 22:7, 29; Mal. 3:5; cf. Ps.

94:6). True religion was inseparable from an ethic of charity toward the disadvantaged (Jer. 7:4–8; Zech. 7:8–10).

Motivations behind laws. What was the reason behind these laws and the prophetic tirades? What would have been the motivation to provide for the needs of these outsiders? The biblical text teaches that one reason for Israel to be gracious was their own history. They, too, had been sojourners many years in Egypt. Unfortunately, that long time as immigrants had degenerated into a period of oppression. Israel was never to forget that experience, and its people were not to repeat the ruthless attitudes and actions of the Egyptians. Consequently, the nation was commanded not to mistreat the sojourner (Exod. 22:21 [22:20 MT]; 23:9). In fact, God calls Israel "aliens and my tenants" (Lev. 25:23). The land is his, and the Israelites are there only by his grace. The LORD was the owner and patron of that territory, and Israel's task was to work it in obedience to his laws. They were his day laborers, as it were, and that truth should define how they dealt with those sojourners who lived among them now.

What is more, the charge to "love your neighbor as yourself" (Lev. 19:18), which Jesus called the second great commandment (Matt. 22:34–40), was extended to the sojourner precisely because of that experience under Pharaoh: "The alien living with you must be treated as one of your native-born. Love him as yourself, for you were aliens in Egypt. I am the LORD your God" (Lev. 19:34). The neighbor to be loved was not to be restricted to family members and other native Israelites. The command points to persons beyond those circles. A proper and edifying mind-set, as well as positive actions toward the immigrant, were expected.

The most serious incentive to care for sojourners was to be found in the person of God. In reminding Israel of its history and the obligations that stemmed from it, the LORD explains that the redemption from their horrific experience as immigrants also revealed something very important about

104

his own person: he loves the helpless, among whom he lists sojourners. Israel, too, is to love sojourners, because God does (Deut. 10:17–19; cf. Ps. 146:6–9). That is why God calls ignoring the cry of these people a sin (Deut. 24:14–15).

Ancient Israel did not have the kind of government we have today, which provides assistance through organized and funded programs. Help for the needy had to occur at several levels: individual families (giving rest on the Sabbath, including sojourners in celebrations), the community (gleaning laws), workplaces of whatever kind (payment of wages), religious centers (collecting of the tithe), and at the city gate with the elders or other legal gatherings (fairness in legal matters). Everyone in a sense was involved somehow in the care of the sojourner. The prophets make clear that God held everyone responsible, from individuals to society as a whole.

> Expectations and responsibilities were placed on sojourners as well.

Assimilation of the sojourner. Through the law we see that Israel opened the most central—and most precious—sphere of its life to sojourners: its religion. This faith was foundational to its identity as a people and marked Israel as different from the surrounding nations. It permeated daily, weekly, monthly, and annual activities and shaped every aspect of its existence. And into this world the sojourner was given entry. Sojourners were permitted to participate in the Sabbath, the Day of Atonement (Lev. 16:29–30), the Passover (Exod. 12:48–49; Num. 9:14), the Feast of Weeks (Deut. 16:11), the Feast of Tabernacles (Deut. 16:14), and Firstfruits (Deut. 26:11). Forgiveness for unintentional sin was extended to them (Num. 15:27–29), and they were afforded access to the cities of refuge (Num. 35:15).

Expectations and responsibilities were placed on sojourners as well. They were to be present at the periodic reading of the law (Deut. 31:10–13). This makes sense. It would be in listening to the law that sojourners could learn more about what it meant to be a member of that society. Listening together with the rest of the people at the Feast of Tabernacles would be a public demonstration of their solidarity with Israel and, in turn, Israel's acceptance of them. This scene also assumes that sojourners speak and understand Hebrew so that they could understand the reading. The language would also be a prerequisite to participating in the other religious and civic activities.

Sojourners were subject to the penalties of criminal laws (Lev. 24:22), many of the dietary restrictions (Exod. 12:19; Lev. 17:10–15), the sexual taboos (Lev. 18:26), purity laws (Num. 19:10), the regulations for the feasts (Num. 9:14; 15:15), and the prohibition against the worship of other gods and blasphemy against the LORD (Lev. 20:1–2; 24:10–16; Num. 15:30–31). A number of these regulations and several of those cited in the preceding paragraph contain the phrase "whether he is a native-born Israelite or an alien." This expresses in another way their equal standing before the law.[18]

Still, some distinctions were made between the native Israelite and the sojourner. For example, there were dietary laws that did not apply to sojourners (Deut. 14:21). There was also reluctance to let foreigners participate at the sanctuary (Deut. 23:3–8), but there are occasions when this rule was ignored. Ruth, obviously, is the stellar example of this, and Solomon's prayer of dedication counters it as well (1 Kings 8:41–43).[19]

Future hope. Finally, there is the prophetic hope that one day the bonding between sojourner and native Israelite would be even closer. Ezekiel 47:21–23 (cf. Isa. 14:1) envisions a time when sojourners will be able to inherit land along with the tribes of Israel. The barrier against possessing their own parcels of the promised land would be done away with. When Isaiah talks of the future ingathering of Israel from exile and depicts their coming to worship at Zion, the holy mountain of God, he includes the "foreigner" (56:1–8; cf.

2:2–4). Interestingly, he uses the term *nokrî*, not *gēr*.[20] These are people from other lands who will come before the LORD, echoing that hope of Solomon in 1 Kings 8:41–43. Foreigner and Israelite together will enjoy his presence in glorious fashion. The breadth of God's mercy and the response of the peoples of the world to his person will not be limited to the native-born or to the boundaries of Israel.

Implications for Today

Different concepts of law. This survey of Old Testament legislation dealing with the sojourner can be instructive in several ways. First of all, the short discussion on law and culture that is informed by cultural anthropology is pertinent. Because Hispanics come from another culture, their concept of law will differ from the way it is understood in this country.

My life has been spent straddling North American Anglo and Latin American cultures. One major difference between these two cultures, to which anyone who has traveled or lived south of the border can attest, is the different appreciation of the meaning and practice of law. This can be empirically verified by anyone at a personal level simply, for instance, by trying to obtain a driver's license, get a visa, pay a fine, conduct a bank transaction, or get a package from a customs house. It quickly becomes apparent that law and laws are inseparable from bureaucratic protocol and artificial (but very important!) formalities, social status, and family connections.

These attitudes and the nature of laws can be traced to a cultural history quite distinct from that of the United States. Latin American law finds its origins on the Iberian peninsula, not in a British heritage. The different branches of government also identify their function and rights in ways that are different from this country, and each branch as well must define itself in relationship to the military establishment (although this has been changing during the past two decades). These and other factors yield a very dissimilar legal culture, which impacts politics and the world of business and their corresponding legal values and structures. In Latin America, all of this is normal and natural; it is the way things have always been, and change comes slowly. Latin America would not be Latin America without this particular flavor of the spice of life. The majority culture should anticipate that the adaptation by immigrants to the laws and legal ethos of the United States will take time. Hispanic immigrants, too, will need to listen to and acquaint themselves with the law of the land (cf. Deut. 31:10–13).

Varied experiences. Second, the Old Testament presents a realistic picture of an ancient society trying to come to grips with a complex social issue. Several terms are applied to outsiders. Even though it is hard to make definite comments about their meanings, the fact that there were multiple types of reference to foreigners in Israel suggests that the experiences with outsiders were varied and that these individuals could be evaluated in different ways. This pattern also is true now of the assessment by the majority culture of other people who have come from a Hispanic culture. In other words, a variety of reactions to the arrival and presence of Hispanic immigrants, today's sojourner, is to be expected.

Law as paradigm. A third point is based on Wright's thesis that the law of Israel is to serve as a paradigm for other nations. It is to be a live illustration of the ethical orientation for life that God intends for all humanity. The next component of this model, which was not mentioned earlier, is Wright's contention that the moral values of Israel's law that found expression in specific regulations relevant to that ancient context are pertinent to the modern era, too. Deuteronomy 4:5–8 points beyond its particular setting. The law is an enduring object lesson. Obviously, the structures, institutions, and other initiatives corresponding to those same values today will look different than they did millennia ago. But God's ethical ideals continue to be valid and should be made concrete in the contemporary world.

Care for the sojourner is one of those ideals. It was a moral demand that set apart God's people from the other nations; even more significantly, it was grounded in God's person. Not to be hospitable, individually or collectively, merited the wrath of the prophets. The law reflects an awareness that sojourners were vulnerable, and so in it are found a series of mechanisms to help meet their physical needs. To this charitable socioeconomic framework is added an invitation to the sojourner into what made Israel, Israel: its religious life.

If what Wright proposes is correct, and I believe it is, then the imperative of caring for the sojourner is also binding today. At the very least, this ethical commitment should resonate with the people of God in the majority culture. It ought to be demonstrated in specific measures that respond to the needs of the immigrant. The means will vary according to the opportunities and limitations in any given context, but the responsibility remains. It also will entail majority-culture Christians and churches opening themselves up and allowing the sojourner admittance to their culture and lives. In addition, if this moral imperative is for all nations, then these Christians have the obligation to be a voice for God's heart in the country at large. Again, the Bible does not provide a blueprint for action, but it does make its call clear.

Identity. In addition to the reality of varied response and the moral imperative, there is yet another lesson to be learned. Care for the sojourner was important for Israel because they, too, had experienced life as sojourners—and that in most unpleasant ways. The rehearsing at the feasts of their history as immigrants in Egypt and the reminder to be gracious to outsiders and the downcast were exercises in collective memory. All of this, ideally, was crucial for their formation as a people of virtue, especially the virtue of generous hospitality. Stated another way, the arrival and presence of sojourners were *not a threat to Israel's national identity;*

rather, their presence was *fundamental to its very meaning.* The people of Israel could not be who they were supposed to be before God and the world if they forgot who they had been and from where they had come.

While the text is speaking about the people of God, there may be an analogy with the United States. Today some deny that this country should be understood as a nation of immigrants. It is said that there have always been restrictions and preferential quotas and that the country has been ambivalent toward those from other lands. This is true, but what this position cannot deny is that every year for over two centuries there has been a flow of immigrants—with or without quotas, with permission or without proper documents—arriving on these shores. The numbers may vary, the color of the faces might change, but the reality of continual immigration is a fact. Immigration is inseparable from the history of the nation and is fundamental to its identity. Every family can point back to parents or grandparents or great grandparents who came from somewhere else. It is part of our familial memory, but at the national level sometimes there is collective amnesia. To deny the past in order to control the present and to shape the future as we would like might be a greater threat to national identity.

Broad responsibility. As mentioned previously, it is interesting to observe that the responsibility to take care of the sojourner in Israel was carried out at many levels, through families, religious centers, and other local initiatives. This was necessitated because of the nature of the ancient context. The modern world is different. Still, while today the government usually is expected to handle such matters, there may be some value in a more multipronged approach that is more inclusive. Wider participation yields deeper social awareness and ethical concern.

Multiple reactions. At least two final lessons are directed more specifically at the immigrant. To begin with, the evidence provided by our discussion on the terminology used to

refer to foreigners in the Old Testament should lead these sojourners to anticipate diverse reactions to their coming here.
Sometimes those who are native-born will qualify foreignness
in a neutral fashion, simply as a label; on other occasions the
foreignness will be considered something negative (and in a
few cases this might be deserved). In the greater number of
instances, however, immigrants may experience the welcome
of the majority culture. In their labors, they may benefit,
too, from the generosity of individuals of the majority culture and the "safety net" afforded by this country's legislation (schooling for children, emergency-room care, and the
like), and myriad independent organizations and Christian
ministries. The problem is that the United States does not
have a law revealed from heaven, and so the legal system
is imperfect and is now being contested and reworked. So,
there are times when the laws will be of assistance and other
times when they could be contradictory, unreasonable, and
unjust. As the process of immigration reform moves forward,
much will depend on the heart of the majority culture, but
there is also a responsibility that the sojourner must accept.
This is the second point.

Cultural accommodation. The Old Testament law makes
clear that there are expectations for the sojourner, just as
there are demands on Israel. Some of the Christian literature
that champions the immigrant draws from the law only a
few verses that command the care of the sojourner. This
could be a strategic decision to convince audiences of the
need to provide for the needy immigrant, and I can appreciate that. But ultimately, such an approach is one-sided and
incomplete. The law assumes that there is movement on the
part of the sojourner toward the host culture (Israel): learning its ways and its language, and respecting its laws and
taboos. There are cases of exemplary foreigners who moved
to and lived within Israel. I have already mentioned Ruth and
Ittai; there are others. What we will never know is to what
extent these individuals accommodated themselves to the

111

culture of Israel and how much of their home culture they retained; most assuredly, it differed for each one. Countless Hispanics are trying to learn the ways of the United States, do appreciate the importance of learning English, and want to be respectful of its customs. I have heard this commitment from Hispanic pastors, who are counseling their people toward these ends. I have seen it in all kinds of persons, who are trying to better their lives here and raise their children in constructive ways. Adaptation is occurring, but how much of home will be retained will depend on a variety of factors relative to each person, family, and community.

Conclusion

Whereas the preceding chapter on the Old Testament highlights the theme of the image of God and then demonstrates just how ubiquitous in the biblical text experiences of living in other countries are, this chapter began with hospitality and then explored the laws regarding the sojourner. Other issues in the Old Testament would be relevant to the immigration debate,[21] but I end my reflections here.

The goal has been to try to uncover a biblical point of view—perhaps, better: a more biblically grounded attitude—toward immigrants and immigration. It is a topic close to the heart of God and inseparable from the life and mission of God's people. Openness to sojourners is a virtue, and concern for their well-being is manifested tangibly in Old Testament law. For their part, sojourners were to respond in positive ways to this invitation to enter the world of Israel.

These truths should help orient how majority culture and Hispanic Christians wrestle with the immigration quandary. With hearts attuned to the will of God, perhaps the tenor of the debate can be leavened with grace and any proposed solutions and compromises guided by divine wisdom. The next chapter will complement what has been presented thus far with the contribution of the New Testament.

4

WELCOMING THE STRANGER

Guidance from the New Testament

Today Jesus comes in many shapes and colors. One has only to go to Google.com on the Internet and enter "images of Jesus" in the search engine and click. Instantly, hundreds of different portrayals of Jesus are available. He appears as Caucasian, African-American, Caribbean, Asian, and Hispanic; he can be meek or manly, pious or warlike, an Eastern Orthodox mystic or a Che Guevara look-alike, a beggar or an entrepreneur who can give guidance to modern CEOs. The possibilities are as varied as the human imagination. Jesus takes on the form of the beholder, amenable to the beholder's own view of life but often missing important dimensions of the portrait of Jesus in the New Testament.

This tendency is true as well in more academic circles. In the past thirty years or so numerous publications have argued that the historical Jesus was not the divine Son of

God of Christian orthodoxy but instead, for example, a peasant cynic or a mystic. The global response to *The Da Vinci Code* and the spectacular claims associated with the Gospel of Judas are evidence of the power that Jesus holds over the general public, but also how fascinated people are with alternative views that reduce Jesus to the merely human. During this same time period more circumspect scholarship has been focusing anew on the Jewish backgrounds of Jesus and the trustworthiness of the Gospel accounts.[1]

This more confident orientation is helpful as we go to the Gospels for insights for the Hispanic immigration debate. How so? What Jesus said and did is real and, if one claims to be a follower of Jesus, these things matter. A better sense of the sociocultural context of his time can also help us better understand any ethical demands he might have made that still have a claim on Christians.

Having said this, though, it is also obvious that Jesus never dealt directly with the topic of immigration per se. While this is true at one level, Jesus did give attention to others who were not Jews or who were marginalized and deemed less valuable as persons (such as women and lepers). If the good news was for all humankind, then Jesus had to expand his disciples' vision to embrace all kinds of people. For his followers and others who heard him, cultural identity was a fundamental issue. If the immigration discussion concerns cultural identity—and it clearly does—then it is important for Christians to see how Jesus dealt with those who were different and to learn from his teaching on such things.

This chapter, therefore, begins with a look at material in the Gospels. I will highlight two of the experiences of Jesus and then discuss two passages of his teaching that are pertinent to our topic. The second section turns to the First Epistle of Peter, which utilizes the language of sojourner in reference to the church. The third section returns to the theme of hospitality that we looked at in chapter 3. The fourth and last section examines Romans 13. This passage brings up the question of legality. Undocumented immigrants have violated laws of the United States, and that inescapable fact, it is said, should be the basis of any treatment of issues concerning immigration. But I have left discussion of Romans 13 for last for a reason. It is the place to end our survey, not the place to begin the conversation.

Learning from Jesus

Jesus the Refugee

Not long after Jesus was born, he and his parents had to leave Bethlehem. The Gospel of Matthew informs us that Herod the Great wanted to kill him (Matt. 2:13–14). Herod had been told by the three magi that they were on their way to see the newborn king of the Jews (2:1–8). Herod was fearful and jealous of any rival to his throne. When the magi did not report back, Herod ordered the slaughter of all the young boys in the area around Bethlehem (2:16–18). This characterization of Herod as paranoid and ruthless fits other portrayals of the king from that period.[2]

Joseph, Mary, and the child Jesus sought asylum in Egypt. There was a large Jewish population in Egypt, especially in Alexandria, so it was natural that they go there. They left in haste after the angel's warning and probably took few possessions with them in order to be able to travel quickly and avoid Herod's troops. There are no details of this sojourn in Egypt, and Matthew is the only Gospel that records it. Apparently, the stay in Egypt was short, perhaps no more than two years. An angel informed the family that Herod had died (2:19–21; 4 BC). They first had wanted to go to their ancestral town, Bethlehem, but

CHRISTIANS AT THE BORDER

Herod's son Archelaus was reigning now over Judea. His reputation for cruelty was reminiscent of his father's (2:22), so Joseph took the family northward and returned once more to Nazareth in Galilee.

The joy of the nativity scene and the wonder of the visit of the magi are overshadowed by the unhappy account of the senseless death of innocent children and the flight of refugees. The migration of this family locates the Jesus story within a movement that spans history, of people desiring a better life or escaping the threat of death.

Jesus and Outsiders

The setting. First-century Palestine was a complicated place.[3] Geographically, it was divided into six principal regions. On the west side of the Dead Sea, the Jordan River, and the Sea of Galilee, from south to north, were Idumea, Judea, Samaria, and Galilee; across the Jordan were Perea and the Decapolis. Politics was a complicated state of affairs. The area was under the overall rule of the Roman Empire, but there was considerable autonomy. Depending on local circumstances and history, the empire appointed regional governors or permitted others, such as Herod the Great, to rule limited kingdoms. In return, Rome expected them to collect taxes, keep the peace, and maintain loyalty to caesar. Palestine was volatile, with strong political rivalries and a vocal population unafraid to appeal to Rome to express their discontent.

The religious world was also very complex. The gods of Greco-Roman religion, the mystery cults, and emperor worship all had their adherents. Divisions within the Jewish faith added yet more color and confusion to the religious landscape. Among the Jews in Judea were several sects, the most significant being the Pharisees, Sadducees, and Essenes. Although the Pharisees were the most influential group in terms of setting the agenda for religious practices,

116

apparently much of the populace did not align itself formally with any one of these groups. Under Herod, Jerusalem had become a world-class city, and pilgrims from all over came to worship at the temple and participate in the Jewish festivals.

Within the region of Samaria resided the Samaritans.[4] They practiced a form of Judaism, but they had a separate holy mountain (Mount Gerizim), their own priesthood, and special beliefs and rituals. They were not accepted as equals by other Jews, and the antipathy between them ran deep. Samaritans were despised because to the Jews they represented a perversion of the faith of Abraham, Isaac, and Jacob. Over the course of centuries the antagonism was marked by a series of betrayals and acts of revenge. In 128 BC the Jewish leader Hyrcanus took over Samaria and burned down the Samaritan sanctuary on Mount Gerizim; in 107 BC he destroyed Shechem. In AD 6/7, during Jesus's youth, Samaritans infiltrated the Passover celebration in Jerusalem and scattered bones in the temple, thereby defiling it. Years later (AD 52), the Samaritans slaughtered a company of pilgrims from Galilee who were on their way to Jerusalem for Passover. This atrocity degenerated into a spiral of violence that led to several interventions by the Romans.

The Samaritans, therefore, were a loathsome people. This hostility is the background for the ministry of Jesus to Samaritans and his appeal to them in his teaching. To do anything charitable for a Samaritan or to say something favorable about them would have been met with dismay by his followers. The disciples' dislike of the Samaritans is illustrated by their reaction to a Samaritan village's rejection of Jesus (Luke 9:51–56). James and John, the "sons of thunder" (Mark 3:17), wanted to call down fire from heaven, perhaps as Elijah had done so many years before, on troops from Samaria (2 Kings 1). To the Jews, the Samaritans were not only religious outsiders; they were enemies. But Jesus would have none of it and rebukes the disciples.

Jesus's personal encounters. The best-known story of Jesus engaging Samaritans is found in the Gospel of John, chapter 4—the account of his conversation with the woman at Jacob's well. This chapter is often cited in discussions about cross-cultural missions, and that can be a suitable appropriation or application of the account.[5] I would like to concentrate, however, more particularly on the significance of Jesus, a rabbi, speaking with a Samaritan, and more specifically, a Samaritan woman. In Jewish tradition Samaritan women were considered to be always unclean; they were categorized as menstruants from the cradle.[6] That this woman is of questionable repute (John 4:16–18) makes Jesus's dialogue with her even more impressive. The extraordinariness of what he does is recognized by the woman herself ("You are a Jew, and I am a Samaritan woman. How can you ask me for a drink?"), and is emphasized by the text's side comment, "For Jews do not associate with Samaritans" (4:9).

At this point in the narrative Jesus is traveling from Judea to Galilee with his disciples. Of course, geographically Samaria lay between the two. It is commonly said that Jesus chose not to take the circuitous route along the eastern side of the Jordan River, which Jews would follow to avoid ritual contamination and confrontation with Samaritans, so that he could have this encounter. Though the decision to take the longer route may have been made by some Jews, other sources tell us that many preferred the shorter, more direct way, even though the trip through Samaria might not be pleasant.[7]

The text says, "Now he *had* to go through Samaria" (4:4). The English "he had" is the translation of the Greek *dei*, an impersonal verb. A literal rendering of the line would be: "Now *it was necessary* for him to go through Samaria" (the same verb appears earlier in 3:7, 14, 30). This was the road required to journey north, but another level of necessity is at work. This occasion was an important part of what Jesus needed to do for his mission. This meeting is not an unplanned, coincidental happenstance. It is part of the predetermined plan of Jesus.

His disciples had gone ahead to buy food, but Jesus sits at the well and waits. The woman arrives alone to draw water. Normally, women would go in groups to do this work. Later we learn that she has not been chaste, so perhaps she would go alone out of shame or because she was shunned by other women. Jesus asks her to serve him some water. This Jewish rabbi was asking a Samaritan woman for help! This was remarkable in its counter-cultural effect. If he were to drink water from a vessel given to him by this woman, Jesus would render himself ritually impure. Jesus, however, does not hesitate. In the give-and-take of their exchange, Jesus leads the woman to consider divine living water (4:10–15) and true worship (vv. 19–24), and at the end Jesus reveals that he is Messiah (vv. 25–26). Although it is impossible to know what the woman actually understood about Jesus at this point, she runs to bring others to hear him (vv. 28–30) and many do believe (vv. 39–42). They are concrete evidence that the harvest indeed is at hand (vv. 34–38)—and it is beginning with Samaritans . . . in Samaria!

Another incident with a Samaritan is found in the Gospel of Luke, chapter 17. Jesus is close to Samaria, verse 11 says, so we do not know if the village he enters was located in Samaria or Galilee. Since Jesus is headed south to Jerusalem, it could very well have been in Samaria. There he hears ten lepers calling out to him (Luke 17:11–13). They stand at a distance, because, according to Jewish purity laws, their disease made them unclean (Lev. 13:45–46; Num. 5:2–3). Jesus tells them to go present themselves to the priests, as stipulated in the law for those who have been cured (Lev. 13:19; 14:1–11). But one of the ten returns to thank him

119

with wonderful humility and gratitude, throwing himself at Jesus's feet in praise to God.

The text then provides information that it has held back until this moment: "and he was a Samaritan" (Luke 17:16). Once more the faith of a Samaritan is exemplary. Jesus underscores the incongruity of being embraced by a Samaritan. He is on his way to the Holy City to be rejected by the Jews, but "this foreigner" believes (17:18). It is possible that Jesus's parting words to the man mean that he alone of the ten achieved full reconciliation with God (17:19).[8]

In both encounters these Samaritan individuals are doubly outcast. To begin with, both are Samaritans. What is more, the first was morally suspect, the second a leper. Jesus transcends the longstanding enmity between the Jews and Samaritans. He accepts the "other," and they accept him. In all of this, Jesus never ceases to be a Jew. Yet, he is able to integrate his cultural core with other transcendent commitments and gracious attitudes that move him beyond the closed society of his peers.

Jesus's teaching. The teaching of Jesus, like his actions, is designed in part to push the boundaries of understanding of his followers. Jesus models a new and different way of looking at persons who are outside the circle of the known and beyond acceptability. He displays this in the way he treats those who are in some sense the marginalized of society—women, the poor, the sick—and those who are outsiders—the Gentiles and Samaritans. What he teaches reinforces and explains that commitment. Two passages are especially relevant. The first deals with a Samaritan, while the second mentions the "stranger" in the context of the final judgment.

> Jesus models a new and different way of looking at persons who are outside the circle of the known and beyond acceptability.

Throughout his ministry Jesus had exchanges with religious leaders. Some had sincere motives and wanted to comprehend God better; others probed Jesus for less noble reasons, trying to trick him into making self-incriminating statements.

The latter appears to be the case in the Gospel of Luke, chapter 10. A scribe ("an expert in the law") rises and confronts Jesus with a question about eternal life (Luke 10:25). Jesus responds with another question that challenges the scribe: "What is written in the law? How do you read it?" (10:26). The scribe answers by saying that one must follow the command to love God (Deut. 6:5) and neighbor (Lev. 19:18). Jesus agrees and commands that he obey those injunctions (Luke 10:27–28).

Something in Jesus's response or tone, however, spurred the scribe to ask a follow-up question: "And who is my neighbor?" He is soliciting a definition as to whom he, as a Jew, should love (10:29). Within that context, the scribe may have been wondering if the neighbor should be limited to his own religious circle or could include any member of the Jewish community. Jesus replies with what is now called the parable of the Good Samaritan (10:30–37).[9]

In this parable, a priest and a levite pass by a man who has been attacked by robbers. The scene and description were very realistic for those days, so the story would have immediately captured the audience's attention. No motive is given for why the religious leaders avoid the injured man. After they depart from the scene, the anticipation would have been that the next person in the story be a common Jew, who would demonstrate a purer, simpler faith. Instead, surprisingly, that person is a Samaritan. The Samaritan not only stops to treat the wounds of the man, but he also takes him to an inn, cares for the man there, and then promises to pay for anything that might be needed in his absence.

The question that had been posed to Jesus was "Who is my neighbor?" The parable complicates what the scribe expected to hear. Whereas the original issue concerned identifying the neighbor the scribe should love, Jesus leaves no doubt in the parable that it is the neighbor who loves, and he loves in very tangible ways. That neighbor, though, is a Samaritan, an enemy and scorned one; *this* is the neighbor who loves! The Samaritan, not the religious leaders (of whom the scribe was one), sets the example. Jesus forces the scribe to acknowledge this truth by asking the obvious question, "Which of the three do you think was a neighbor . . . ?" The scribe responds correctly, but he cannot bring himself to say "the Samaritan." The merciful person is simply called "the one" (10:36).

Jesus concludes their exchange by telling the scribe to emulate that neighbor, the Samaritan, in order to fulfill the command to love (10:37). Once again, the people of God are taught about true faith through an encounter with one outside and rejected by their culture.

The second passage is the discourse of Matthew 25:31–46. This is part of the longer exchange between Jesus and his disciples on the Mount of Olives not too long before the crucifixion (Matt. 24:1–25:46). In these verses Jesus speaks about the final judgment of the nations of the world. This passage draws on imagery from the Old Testament and other Jewish literature.[10] In those texts God usually functions as the judge, but there are cases where judgment is performed by another end-time figure he appoints. Here that individual is the Son of Man, who acts in the name of his Father. The divine decision regarding merited eternal blessing and eternal judgment are based on how people have treated the Son of Man/King and the "least of these brothers of mine."

These verses are relevant to the immigration discussion because of the use of the word "stranger" (or "foreigner," Greek *xenos*) in Matthew 25:35, 38, 43, and 44. This term is included with the hungry, thirsty, naked, sick, and imprisoned, and all of these are called the "least of these brothers of mine" (25:40, 45). Some believe that this listing of those

122

who suffer, along with the stranger, shows the breadth of Jesus's concern for the needy and emphasizes the ethical demand placed on all humankind. To ignore any of these people, these "little ones," is tantamount to refusing Jesus himself.[11] Since the stranger is one of them, here we have the moral imperative to take care of the immigrant.

At first glance, this interpretation is attractive, but it cannot withstand careful scrutiny. In the Gospel of Matthew "little ones" refers to the disciples of Jesus (10:42; 18:6, 10, 14), as do his "brothers" (except when the reference is to earthly siblings).[12] This passage, therefore, speaks of the hardships of disciples, the messengers of the gospel, and their treatment by the nations.[13] The theme of their reception as they go out in Jesus's name appeared earlier in the ministry of the Twelve (10:11–42). To scorn the disciples and their message is to reject Jesus, the one who is the essence of that message and who sends the disciples. Their future itinerant ministry would make them "strangers" wherever they go. Accordingly, Matthew 25:31–46 sets the stage for the commission to go to the world in 28:16–20. In his epistles, Paul makes frequent mention of the many hardships in his travels, and the apostle publicly commends those who receive him graciously (e.g., 1 Cor. 16:5–9; Gal. 4:13–14; cf. 3 John 5–10) and encourages others to do the same (e.g., Rom. 16:1–2; 1 Cor. 16:10–12).

Implications for Today

No direct teaching. This brief survey confirms that there is no explicit teaching on immigration in the Gospels. What this does *not* mean, however, is that there is nothing relevant to the immigration discussion.

To begin with, one of the few incidents that are mentioned about the childhood of Jesus is that he and his family were refugees. They flee to another country for safety. On the one hand, this account, as we saw with other migration stories in the Old Testament, provides those who have had to emigrate from their homeland a point of special connection to the text. Aspects of their own situation and experiences are analogous to the details of this story of Jesus.[14] On the other hand, sometimes those who have been able to live stable lives and pursue careers and raise their families in peace and comfort in one place may not be able to sense the power of this account of Jesus in the same way.

The "stranger" and the separation of the sheep and goats at the final judgment may not apply directly to the topic of immigration, but at second glance an important admonition could be suggested there. In chapter 1 it was pointed out that within the Hispanic community—those who have been here for generations as well as more recent immigrants, whether documented or undocumented—are many millions of Christians. In the Matthew passage the "stranger" is technically a disciple who goes to another land for ministry and thus is a foreigner there. I do not make a one-to-one correspondence between the disciples of Matthew 25 and all Hispanic immigrants, but it does seem to me that the care of disciples Jesus demands is pertinent to some extent. Many Hispanic believers who come as immigrants are needy. Does the Christian church of the host culture not have some responsibility to help "the least of these brothers" in the name of Jesus? Does not Christ dwell among and in them, too? Would this revelation that the judgment on the nations is based in part on the treatment of disciples have any application to the United States? Will the Son of Man and the Father in any way demand an accounting of this country's actions toward Christian Hispanics?[15]

Encountering the outsider. There is much to be gleaned for immigration discussions from the way Jesus deals with Samaritans, both in his personal ministry and in his teaching. The Samaritans were culturally different from the Jews; they were despised and discriminated against. Jesus turns these attitudes on their heads by having direct contact with Samaritans (one a woman and the other a leper) and using a Samaritan in a parable. In all of these passages, Samaritans are models of genuine relationship with God. Jesus does and says these things as a member of the majority culture of his time.

A key issue today concerns how the majority culture in the US perceives national cultural identity and its maintenance in light of the growing presence of Hispanics. This is a natural concern, even though, as we explained in the first chapter, it is more complicated than many think. The point here is that Jesus confronts the identity question head on through what he does with Samaritans. Even as he continues to live as a Jew, Jesus lays aside the exclusivistic mores and negative feelings of his cultural heritage toward Samaritans for more important things: their value as persons and the potential of their faith. Jesus gives worth, hope, and direction to a woman who has had a rough life; he heals a leper and brings him joy and a future.

> Jesus's actions and attitudes transcend cultural identity; they also help define what it means to be his follower.

Jesus's actions and attitudes transcend cultural identity; they also help define what it means to be his follower. To stress this is not to deny the many contributions of culture or the importance of a specific identity, but it does put these concerns into perspective. Perhaps these things have to be held a bit more loosely, so that we can have the freedom to engage those from other backgrounds and cultures. Of course, these same comments are directed at Hispanics and Hispanic culture(s), too. Hispanics also are wrestling with cultural maintenance and change. This was a major topic in chapter 1. All of us must learn from Jesus.

The bigger picture. Jesus's treatment of the Samaritans is but one piece of his proactive consideration of those who were marginalized in his society.[16] It is one dimension of a larger set of ethical commitments. He reaches out to the poor, the sick, women, sinners of all kinds, Gentiles, and Samaritans. In light of this truth, a fundamental question must be asked. Does what Jesus did and said have any relevance for Christians today? Is he simply our Savior, one to whom we turn in faith for eternal redemption? Or, in addition to our personal salvation, is his life a model for all time of how to live a life that pleases God and reflects his character on earth? In a sense, we are returning to the dialogue between the Jewish scribe and Jesus. What does God require of those who claim to be believers?

If the life and words of Jesus in some fashion are important and binding on Christians, then other questions follow. Do we, as Christians, have as comprehensive an ethic as Jesus had? If not, why not? What areas of life have been left out? Have attitudes and actions toward Hispanics been integrated into that ethic? Along with what are normally highlighted as Christian duties, such as honesty in the workplace, fidelity in marriage, and good stewardship of money, must also stand compassion toward the outsider.

These next two sections are briefer than this one on the Gospels. Each in some way builds off discussions from previous chapters. The first section below looks at the use of sojourner vocabulary in the First Epistle of Peter, and the one that follows revisits the theme of hospitality.

Christians as Sojourners

1 Peter

The terminology of the sojourner appears several times in the First Epistle of Peter.[17] The recipients of the letter are called "strangers" (*parepidēmos*) in 1:1,[18] and "aliens and strangers" (*paroikos* and *parepidēmos*) in 2:11. In the Greco-Roman world these words referred to foreigners who had moved into the area to reside there. A "stranger" was a more transient resident than was the "alien." These foreigners were not granted the rights and privileges of full citizenship, and so they had to endure economic, political, and social limitations. Because they were different, they were not always welcome in their new home.

Commentators disagree in what sense these (and by extension all) Christians are "strangers." Based on other New Testament texts, some argue that all believers have their ultimate citizenship in heaven. We are foreigners in this fallen world who are journeying on to our celestial home (cf. Phil. 3:20; Heb. 13:14). The apostle Paul also uses this vocabulary to speak of Gentile Christians, who in the past had been separated from the people of God but are now brought into the household of faith through faith in Christ (Eph. 2:19).

The context of the letter, however, strongly suggests that these Christians are "strangers" in a way different from these two options. Some light is available through the phrase "aliens and strangers" in 2:11. This exact combination of words appears in only one other place in the Septuagint (i.e., the Greek Old Testament): Genesis 23:4. This is the passage where Abraham buys land from Ephron the Hittite to bury his wife Sarah. This Old Testament allusion connects the experience of these Christians back to the ancient patriarch. Their sojourning is not unique. The history of the people of God is the pilgrimage of faith of those who are alienated from the world. Abraham's sojourning was literal. He was an outsider without land or roots in the region in which he had settled. If the patriarch's sojourn was something concrete, then perhaps that of these first-century believers was as well. In what sense, then, were they "aliens and strangers"?

Whether these Christians (or a portion of them) were sojourners in the Greco-Roman sense before their conversion or whether they were expelled or exiled from another place in the Empire is impossible to say.[19] If actual experiences did determine this choice of words, then they would have had quite an impact. Unquestionably, though, all of them now were outsiders in their world because of their distinct lifestyle and their allegiance to Jesus. Their spiritual life wrought a different social life, one that their neighbors were critical of. The letter repeatedly exhorts its readers to endure persecution and to live a life of holiness, humility, and integrity. As they maintained their good testimony, unbelievers would take notice and some would acknowledge God (2:12, 15; 3:1–2, 16).

Implications for Today

There are at least two lessons that 1 Peter offers Christians engaged in the immigration discussion. The first lesson is *not* that since all Christians are "aliens and strangers" then majority culture Christians should accept immigrants. To make that claim on the basis of this passage misses its intent. The epistle teaches that all Christians are aliens and strangers because of their distinct set of commitments and values vis-à-vis the society in which we live.

From this perspective, if majority culture Christians embrace the immigrant—whether documented or undocumented—they would be aliens and strangers in that they would be going against the current of a good portion of public opinion. To take that stand on the basis of biblical convictions may lead to opposition from the broader majority culture. According to 1 Peter, to suffer for doing good is a privilege and part of the pilgrimage of faith.

Once again, all Christians, those of the majority and Hispanic cultures, are aliens and strangers in the world because of their faith. This is something they share. But there is another point here, and it echoes what has been mentioned earlier. Immigrant believers might identify with details of this biblical text through their analogous experiences.

Immigrants are aliens and strangers in this country in a physical, cultural, and social sense, too. Consequently, they can face rejection and discrimination at this level, not just at the faith level. This second dimension of their experience as aliens and strangers can add a richness to their reading of the epistle. If the hypotheses that suggest that the original recipients of the letter were actually social outcasts are correct, then the Hispanic experience is close to what those early Christians went through; Hispanics may hear the apostle's words in a manner similar to its original audience. In these ways, Hispanic Christians might be able to contribute to the majority culture Christians' understanding of the exhortations and promises of the Word of God.

The Call to Hospitality

New Testament Teaching

Chapter 3, the second part of our survey of the Old Testament, began with a discussion of hospitality in the ancient world and Israel. The practice of hospitality continued into the first century and beyond. In the New Testament, hospitality received an even greater impetus and was a prominent custom in the early church. Meals were shared and shelter provided to Christians and non-Christians, to friends, family, and strangers.[20]

In addition to the many examples of hospitality that can be found in the New Testament, the words of Jesus and exhortations in several letters are sources of teaching on the subject. The Gospel accounts describe a number of scenes where Jesus is in someone's home for a meal (a well-known example is the dinner party at Zacchaeus's house, Luke 19:1–10), but the teaching Jesus gives at a meal in a Pharisee's house in the Gospel of Luke, chapter 14, is the most relevant. When Jesus sees how guests at this dinner vie

129

for places of prominence, he tells his host that the special guests at a banquet in God's sight would be the poor and the sick, those of no social standing who would not have the means to repay the gesture (Luke 14:12–14). Many verses urge Christians to offer a gracious welcome to others. These include Romans 12:13, Hebrews 13:2 (undoubtedly an allusion to Genesis 18 and 19), and 1 Peter 4:9. The virtue of hospitality was expected of the leadership of the Christian community (1 Tim. 3:2; Titus 1:8; cf. 1 Tim. 5:9–10).[21]

The early church gathered in homes to enjoy fellowship, meet their physical needs, and share meals. These small assemblies in an intimate context were a good setting for the practice of hospitality. The most profound opportunity to embody hospitality was the celebration of the Lord's Supper. This meal is grounded in the sacrifice of Jesus on the cross and is rooted in his final meal with the disciples. If hospitality is about opening oneself up and giving oneself to others, then the conjunction of the Lord's Supper and the cross are a powerful demonstration of divine hospitality. All are welcome. It is no wonder that Paul's instruction on the Lord's Supper in 1 Corinthians 11 combines concern for the unfortunate with the call to serious self-evaluation (11:17–34). The Lord's Supper, so central a symbol of the Christian faith and so important for nurturing the remembrance of the work of Christ, was inseparable from the practice of hospitality.

Implications for Today

There is no need for me to add much more at this point to what has already been said in the previous chapter concerning hospitality and its relationship to the immigration discussion. The New Testament reinforces the importance and value of hospitality with what Jesus said and did and with the numerous directives in the epistles. Of course, for the Christian the Lord's Supper is the consummate reminder of the need to be hospitable to others, even to those very different from ourselves, to the stranger in our midst.

What about Romans 13?

Why Romans 13 Now?

I have placed this New Testament text last by design. In conversations I have had with students, friends, and others, Romans 13:1–7 is often brought up to argue against allowing entry to undocumented Hispanic immigrants. To cross the border without the proper permission, it is said, is to break the law of the United States. Their presence in this country by definition, therefore, is illegal. In its crassest form, I have heard this as, "What is it about 'illegal' that you don't understand?" This wrong of violating the nation's borders should be sanctioned, and these lawbreakers should expect to suffer the consequences. Moreover, how can Hispanics who claim to be Christians so blatantly violate a clear teaching of Scripture?

If one begins here, any sensible discussion about Hispanic immigration is quickly aborted. It is my conviction that there are a series of prior considerations that must be dealt with before introducing issues of legality. One must treat legal matters eventually. The country needs to make some decisions and to organize itself on these issues. Responses to the challenges of immigration, however, should arise from a set of beliefs and commitments. For the Christian, these ultimately must be grounded in the Bible. That is why this book is structured the way it is and why this passage has not been considered until now.

If one begins with a biblical orientation that includes the centrality of the importance of the immigrant as made in the image of God, if one can appreciate how pervasive migration experiences are to the history and faith of the people of

God, if Old Testament law projects an ethics of compassion, if the thrust of Jesus's ministry and the New Testament as a whole is to love the outsider and be hospitable, then the inclination is to be gracious to the immigrant in the name of God and Christ. This inclination, in turn, will affect how one assesses present legislation and ponders where things should go from here at a personal level, in the local and national church and other Christian spheres, and finally within the country at every level of government.

If, on top of these faith convictions, one evaluates the history of immigration law in the United States as confused, contradictory, and in some ways unfair to the various affected parties, then that also will affect the perspective on the legality question. If one believes that these laws do not fit the teaching of the Bible and the ethical demands of the heart of God, some Christians will not say "What is it about 'illegal' that you don't understand?"; instead, they might declare with the apostles Peter and John: "Judge for yourselves whether it is right in God's sight to obey you rather than God" (Acts 4:19).

Before this statement raises all kinds of alarm, let me make it very clear that I am not advocating civil disobedience on a large scale, just as most Christians who have strong misgivings about undocumented immigrants are not lobbying for a massive national deportation operation to rid the country of one and all. It is a narrow understanding of the nature of law and the Christian's relationship to human government that I question.

The Problem with Romans 13

Many Christians read Romans 13 with the assumption that all the nation's laws are inherently good and just. To obey them is then not only pleasing to God, it is common sense.[22] What can be missed is that Romans 12, which prefaces Paul's words concerning human government, contrasts the mind-set and life of Christians with what they encounter in society. Romans 12 exhorts believers not to be shaped by the "pattern of this world"; they should serve others, show love and have compassion, and help their enemies (Rom. 12:3–21).

The government has a different agenda and set of rules. The Christian should respect that fact, but this does not mean sanctifying everything a human government decrees and does. One of the wonderful privileges that the political system of the United States allows is the right to disagree with the government. Motivated by their principles, Christians do this all the time in multiple ways: at the ballot box; through publications; by organizing educational, legal, and civic organizations that would defend other points of view; by participating in peaceful protests of many kinds for a host of causes. I could go on. Each of these actions in its own way expresses reservations about the state of affairs and the things the government is mandating.

> The US government itself recognizes that it must change its legislation.

The US government itself recognizes that it must change its legislation. The national leadership from across the political spectrum and the country as a whole know that what is in place now is not working and must be revised or replaced. The various recent attempts to craft a comprehensive immigration policy are evidence of the need for new laws on immigration.

Therefore, to quote Romans 13 on the immigration issue without nuance or biblical and historical depth simply will not do. I am arguing that all Christians should search the Scriptures for guidance in evaluating the development of immigration policy and engaging its multifaceted set of problems. From that foundation, Christians could begin to move forward to the legal issues. Discussion on legality cannot be limited just to questions about complying with the present laws. If the laws are problematic theologically,

133

humanely, and pragmatically—and since everyone agrees that reform must come—the call to submit to the authorities in Romans 13 can be processed in fresh and constructive ways. Respect for the nation's present laws is coupled with and informed by the move toward a new set of laws. As Christians participate in this change, in whatever fashion, they should do so self-consciously *as Christians*.

Immigrants and Romans 13

In closing, I would like to offer some observations concerning how Hispanic believers, who are undocumented immigrants, respond to Romans 13. Of course, there would be those that set aside the passage on exegetical, theological, and pastoral grounds. My experience, however, is with Hispanic Christians primarily of the evangelical and Pentecostal streams. They would take this biblical text seriously, but their view is complex.

These Christians recognize that they are in violation of the law by living and working here. At the same time, they have experienced personally the law's contradictions and inequities. For example, the government turns a blind eye to many employers because the country needs the cheap labor, but then closes the door to social services on these same workers. They also respect the legal system of the United States for its efficiency and fairness in many areas. Many pay taxes, and they do their best to obey the laws of the land in every area that does not threaten their jobs, homes, and children's education. I have heard many express a desire to be model "citizens" as part of their Christian duty and in order to gain the respect of the majority culture. Finally, all wish for a legal resolution of the situation. That is, their hope is that the law itself will be reformed in such a way that their legal status is no longer an issue.

5

WHERE DO WE GO FROM HERE?

Final Thoughts

Hispanic immigration to the United States is a complex phenomenon. It has a history that extends back over 150 years. This history is not only about the movement of people across borders; it is also the story of complicated legislation and diverse cultural reactions. The number of immigrants, documented and undocumented, who have entered the country during the past thirty years has made this phenomenon the focus of national debate at many levels and in all sorts of arenas. This debate can be heated, and it has generated interesting alliances that cross traditional ideological lines. Those who favor more restrictive immigration policies are nativists, environmentalists, low-skilled laborers who feel threatened, some unions, and citizens fearful about national security, the economic viability of social services, and the future of the reigning cultural identity. Those who favor a more open strategy include free-market thinkers, business and agricultural interests, the AFL-CIO, human rights organizations and activists, and much of academia. Strange bedfellows indeed!

Christians, of course, are members of this society and locate themselves at different points along this broad spectrum of opinion. When I have engaged Christians in conversation about immigration, I have found that more often than not this choice has had little to do with Christian convictions and much to do with ideological commitments and personal background and experience. This book attempts to offer what appears to be lacking: a biblical and theological framework from which Christians, *as Christians*, might participate in the ongoing debate.

At Two Borders

As I explained in the introduction, the title *Christians at the Border* carries two meanings. On the one hand, Christians in the United States all stand at the border with Mexico in a sociopolitical and economic sense. Everyone needs to make a decision about a host of concrete realities related to Hispanic immigration. That decision will influence how one treats Hispanics in the encounters of everyday life and how one expresses that point of view in the political arena. To meet the need to be informed about these kinds of issues, chapter 1 outlines a history of Hispanic immigration and summarizes the principal arguments revolving around two of the more salient issues: cultural identity and the economic impact of immigration. These topics are broader and more intricate than many suppose, so the chapter presents additional perspectives on these two issues and then closes by including a third that often is ignored: Hispanic Christianity.

WHERE DO WE GO FROM HERE?

Among Hispanic immigrants are millions of believers, so a Christian consideration of the national debate must take account of their presence.

The imposing array of problems and challenges should drive Christians to seek the wisdom of God. Chapters 2 through 4, then, survey the relevant biblical material. These chapters do not pretend to be exhaustive nor is the discussion (hopefully!) overly technical. My goal has been to demonstrate to the reader the wealth of divine revelation relevant to the topic of immigration. Chapter 2 begins with a discussion of the image of God and subsequently cites a multitude of passages that portray migrants in the Old Testament. Chapter 3 continues in the Old Testament, moving from a consideration of the theme of hospitality to a treatment of Old Testament law. Chapter 4 turns to the New Testament. It begins with the experiences and teaching of Jesus and then briefly deals with the phrase "aliens and strangers" in 1 Peter, revisits the theme of hospitality, and responds to objections that may arise from a particular interpretation of Romans 13.

Throughout these chapters, the biblical presentations are followed by a section called "Implications for Today." The purpose of these reflections is to attempt to put the Bible and the situation of Hispanic immigration in dialogue. The survey of biblical material and these reflections place Christians at another, metaphorical, border. We must *all* make a decision about how to respond to the Bible's teaching and the example of Jesus. There is a threshold to cross, a road of obedience to travel.

If crossing that border transforms how majority-culture Christians view immigrants and immigration, and if it shapes how immigrants understand their life, privileges, and responsibilities in this country, then this crossing leads all back to that first border. The political boundary with Mexico now takes on a greater significance at the boundary of faith.

The Purpose of This Book

There is much this book does not cover. The sphere of the social, political, and economic is huge. The opening chapter is simply a doorway into these vast realms of data, opinions, and policy. The scope of the biblical discussion can also be daunting. The endnotes for each chapter and the appendix are designed to refer the interested reader to other resources.

This book also does not propose any legislative solutions, economic panaceas, or advice on cultural negotiations. *Christians at the Border* above all else strives to motivate believers of the majority culture and Hispanics to begin thinking, talking, and acting *as Christians* in regard to immigration. What I have written here is a starter, a primer. I do not aspire to anything more. If, through the grace of God it can stimulate biblical and theological reflection, then it will have served its purpose.

Final Thoughts

Resident Aliens is the provocative title of a stimulating work on Christian identity and ministry in modern America by Stanley Hauerwas and William Willimon.[1] The idea behind the title apparently comes from one of the biblical quotations that preface the book: "But our citizenship is in heaven" (Phil. 3:20–21). The title is apropos to our concerns, as "resident aliens" is one of the translations given for the Hebrew and Greek words of the Bible that refer to the sojourner. *Resident Aliens*, however, does not deal at all with immigration issues (it was published in 1989). Nevertheless, what it says is relevant.

Hauerwas and Willimon's contention is that the Christian church has lost its way and is captive to the culture. The church must regain the vision of being a distinct community, a distinct community made up of ordinary individuals with a calling to be faithful to its Lord. The focus on living the life of the Savior in the world is clear from the other biblical quotation that begins their book: "Your attitude should be the same as that of Christ Jesus" (Phil. 2:5). Christians are to display the life of Jesus, and this requires acquiring a set of virtues, like peaceableness, kindness, hospitality, and patience. Christians and the church need to be a certain kind of people with a particular way of looking at and living within society. For the church to be the church requires training in these virtues, the nurturing of Christian tradition through Word and sacrament, and the continual practice of the virtues.

> An appropriate response to the complicated situation in society will not come from detached, objective analysis, cost-benefit calculations, efficiency quotients, and cultural arguments.

The virtues are fundamental for a Christian approach to Hispanic immigration.[2] An appropriate response to the complicated situation in society will not come from detached, objective analysis, cost-benefit calculations, efficiency quotients, and cultural arguments. The decisions that are made and courses of action that are recommended should be commensurate with the life of Jesus—his actions, his teaching, his cross. Analysis and calculations are necessary, but they must be informed by more transcendent beliefs and other overriding life commitments.

Christians, both of the majority culture and Hispanic, are not to exclude the "other," whether Christian or non-Christian.[3] We are all called to embrace the "other." We can embrace those who are different—and even those who have offended or wronged us—because we have embraced Jesus, who calls us to a self-sacrificing life for others. We embrace him, because he first embraced us. We take up that cross of forgiveness and hospitality because he took up his.

139

This embrace of the other—the majority culture of the Hispanic and the Hispanic of the majority culture—will be a "soft embrace." Resident aliens will embrace resident aliens: respectful and mindful of differences, open to grow and change, reciprocal and mutual, personal and communal, assured yet with great risk, while confident in the light of the Word, the empowerment of the Spirit, the example of Jesus, and the blessing of the Father. Let the journey to reconciliation begin. May the church lead the way.

AFTERWORD

Ronald J. Sider
Palmer Theological Seminary and
Evangelicals for Social Action

There is no denying that the plight of undocumented immigrants is one of the thorniest issues on our national landscape in 2008. It provokes very heated debates. How refreshing it is, then, to have Daniel Carroll R., an author who is sympathetic to both the immigrant and the host culture, call Christians to find a fresh starting point for the debate.

Carroll rightly reminds us of the complexities of the historical, cultural, and economic dimensions of immigration. These dimensions give rise to much of the rhetoric we hear today (from both sides). But Carroll is absolutely right to insist that for Christians there is an even more important dimension that must be considered—that of our Christian faith. Many of the millions who have crossed America's southern border in recent years, with or without proper documentation, are Christians. Surely the faith of the immigrants and the faith of Christians in the host culture must be decisive in the way churches, communities, and individual believers think about and respond to the political and social realities of the current immigration crisis.

The Bible is the most important place to look for guidance. I agree with Carroll that Christians—both immigrants and those in the majority culture—must look at the issue through biblical lenses. Those lenses remind us first of all that these debates are about people—people made in the image of God, with all the inherent worth and standing that lofty designation entails. Policy debates, statistics, spreadsheets, and economic outcomes can often cloud this simple fact that we must ever keep before us.

As we look in the Old Testament, we are reminded of the people of God who many times crossed national boundaries. We also see plentiful evidence of God's persistent and profound love for the needy and the disenfranchised. The biblical record also shows how the people of God lived out their faith while sojourning and how God legislated the behavior of outsiders who came to live with his people. The Old Testament record, then, speaks to both populations, calling for hospitality, grace, and faith as we think and work together toward political and economic solutions.

As we move to the New Testament and the life of Jesus, we see his ongoing example of proactive consideration for the marginalized in society, the outsiders. Later in the New Testament, 1 Peter confronts us with the fact that all Christians are "aliens and strangers" in this world because of their faith. We must, therefore, look at societal issues differently. We're not driven primarily by political or economic expediencies or by partisan rhetoric but by a new set of values, a kingdom way of living on planet earth. Our citizenship in heaven transcends the differences in our earthly nationalities. As Christians think about Hispanic immigration, our approach must be grounded in that citizenship. And the courses of action we recommend must be in line with biblical teaching.

The final chapter title asks where we go from here. Let's follow Danny Carroll in going to the Bible. Let's join him in thinking biblically and theologically about this issue of great national import. Let's find distinctively Christian approaches to meeting such obvious human needs. Let's energize our churches and our communities, finding ways to work toward practices and policies that honor the dignity of every human and that demonstrate the love of God to all who observe our words and actions.

APPENDIX

SELECTED RESOURCES

T he amount of literature on immigration is exploding, and the Internet sites dedicated to issues concerning immigration continue to multiply. By necessity, what follows is limited to *a selection* of this burgeoning number of resources. Since this listing cannot be exhaustive, I have tried to make it representative of different viewpoints. I also have limited the following to resources in English. Additional resources appear in the notes.

Sociological, Economic, and Political Studies

Barone, Michael. *The New Americans: How the Melting Pot Can Work Again*. Washington, DC: Regnery, 2001.

Borjas, George J., ed. *Mexican Immigration to the United States*. National Bureau of Economic Research Conference Report. Chicago: University of Chicago Press, 2007.

Buchanan, Patrick J. *State of Emergency: The Third World Invasion and Conquest of America*. New York: Thomas Dunne, 2006.

Cohen, Jeffrey. *The Culture of Migration in Southern Mexico*. Austin: University of Texas Press, 2004.

Fox, Vicente, with Rob Allyn. *Revolution of Hope: The Life, Faith, and Dreams of a Mexican President*. New York: Viking, 2007.

Haerens, Margaret, ed. *Illegal Immigration: Opposing Viewpoints*. Opposing Viewpoints Series. Detroit: Thomson Gale, 2006.

Hanson, Gordon H. *Why Does Immigration Divide America? Public Finance and Political Opposition to Open Borders*. Washington, DC: Institute for International Economics, 2005.

Hanson, Victor Davis. *Mexifornia: A State of Becoming*. San Francisco: Encounter Books, 2003.

Hatton, Timothy J., and Jeffrey G. Williamson. *Global Migration and the World Economy: Two Centuries of Policy and Performance*. Cambridge, MA: MIT Press, 2005.

Higham, John. *Strangers in the Land: Patterns of American Nativism, 1860–1925*. 2nd rev. ed. New Brunswick, NJ: Rutgers University Press, 2002.

Huntington, Samuel P. *Who Are We? The Challenges to America's National Identity*. New York: Simon & Schuster, 2004.

Laufer, Peter. *Wetback Nation: The Case for Opening the Mexican-American Border*. Chicago: Ivan R. Lee, 2004.

Massey, Douglas S., Jorge Durand, and Nolan J. Malone. *Beyond Smoke and Mirrors: Mexican Immigration in an Era of Economic Integration*. New York: Russell Sage Foundation, 2002.

Miles, Ann. *From Cuenca to Queens: An Anthropological Story of Transnational Migration*. Austin: University of Texas Press, 2004.

Nevins, Joseph. *Operation Gatekeeper: The Rise of the "Illegal Alien" and the Remaking of the U.S.-Mexico Boundary*. New York: Routledge, 2001.

Portes, Alejandro, and Rubén G. Rumbaut. *Immigrant America: A Portrait*. 3rd ed. Berkeley: University of California Press, 2006.

Pritchett, Lant. *Let Their People Come: Breaking the Gridlock on Global Labor Mobility*. Washington, DC: Center for Global Development, 2006.

145

Smith, Robert Courtney. *Mexican New York: Transnational Lives of New Immigrants*. Berkeley: University of California Press, 2006.

Tancredo, Tom. *In Mortal Danger: The Battle for America's Border and Security*. Nashville: WND Books, 2006.

Zolberg, Aristide R. *A Nation by Design: Immigration Policy in the Fashioning of America*. New York: Russell Sage Foundation; Cambridge, MA: Harvard University Press, 2007.

Hispanic Experience: Crossing the Border and Life in the United States (Autobiography, Reporting, and Realistic Cultural Fiction)

Álvarez, Julia. *How the García Girls Lost Their Accent*. New York: Plume, 1992.

———. *Once upon a Quinceañera: Coming of Age in the U.S.A.* New York: Viking, 2007.

Chávez, Linda. *Out of the Barrio: Toward a New Politics of Hispanic Assimilation*. New York: Basic Books, 1991.

Cisneros, Sandra. *Caramelo or Puro Cuento*. New York: Vintage, 2002.

Martínez, Rubén. *Crossing Over: A Mexican Family on the Migrant Trail*. New York: Metropolitan Books, 2001.

Paz Soldán, Edmundo. *The Matter of Desire*. Translated by Lisa Carter. Boston: Houghton Mifflin, 2001.

Ramos, Jorge. *Dying to Cross: The Worst Immigrant Tragedy in American History*. Translated by K. Cordero. New York: Rayo, 2005.

———. *The Other Face of America: Chronicles of the Immigrants Shaping Our Future*. Translated by P. J. Duncan. New York: Rayo, 2002.

Rodríguez, Richard. *Brown: The Last Discovery of America*. New York: Penguin, 2002.

Stavans, Ilan. *The Hispanic Condition: Reflections on Culture and Identity in America*. New York: HarperCollins, 1995.

————. *Latino History and Culture*. New York: HarperCollins, 2007.

Urrea, Luis Alberto. *The Devil's Highway: A True Story*. New York: Back Bay Books, 2004.

Villaseñor, Victor. *Burro Genius: A Memoir*. New York: HarperCollins, 2004.

Biblical and Theological Resources

Biblical and Theological Studies

Bietenhard, H., and F. S. Rothenberg. "Foreign, Alien, Dispersion, Stranger." In *The New International Dictionary of New Testament Theology*. Edited by Colin Brown, vol. 1, 683–92. Grand Rapids: Zondervan, 1975.

Block, Daniel I. "Sojourner." In *International Standard Bible Encyclopaedia*. Edited by G. W. Bromiley, vol. 4, 561–64. Rev. ed. Grand Rapids: Eerdmans, 1988.

Ekblad, Bob. *Reading the Bible with the Damned*. Louisville: Westminster John Knox, 2005.

Escobar, Samuel. "Immigration: Avenue and Challenge to Mission." *Journal of Latin American Theology* 1, no. 2 (2006): 70–94.

Gowan, Donald E. "Wealth and Poverty in the Old Testament: The Case of the Widow, the Orphan, and the Sojourner." *Interpretation* 41, no. 4 (1987): 341–53.

Griffin, Mark, and Theron Walker. *Living on the Borders: What the Church Can Learn from Ethnic Immigrant Cultures*. Grand Rapids: Brazos, 2004.

Kellermann, D. "*gûr*." In *Theological Dictionary of the Old Testament*. Edited by G. J. Botterweck and H. Ringgren, vol. 2, 439–49. Grand Rapids: Eerdmans, 1975.

Knauth, R. J. D. "Alien, Foreign Resident." In *Dictionary of the Old Testament: Pentateuch*. Edited by T. Desmond Alexander and David W. Baker, 26–33. Downers Grove, IL: InterVarsity, 2003.

147

Miller, Patrick D. "Israel as Host to Strangers." In *Israelite Religion and Biblical Theology: Collected Essays*, edited by Patrick D. Miller, 548–71. Journal for the Study of the Old Testament Supplement Series 267. Sheffield: Sheffield Academic Press, 2000.

O'Neil, William R., and William C. Spohn. "Rights of Passage: The Ethics of Immigration and Refugee Policy." *Theological Studies* 59, no. 1 (1998): 84–106.

Pohl, Christine D. "Biblical Issues in Mission and Migration." *Missiology: An International Review* 31, no. 1 (2003): 3–15.

———. "Responding to Strangers: Insights from the Christian Tradition." *Studies in Christian Ethics* 19, no. 1 (2006): 81–101.

Ramírez Kidd, José E. *Alterity and Identity in Israel: The Ger in the Old Testament*. Beihefte zur Zeitschrift für die alttestamentliche Wissenschaft 283. Berlin: de Gruyter, 1999.

Rendtorff, R. "The *Ger* in the Priestly Laws of the Pentateuch." In *Ethnicity and the Bible*, edited by Mark G. Brett, 77–87. Biblical Interpretation Series. Leiden: Brill, 1996.

Schmidt, K. L., M. A. Schmidt, and R. Meyer. "*paroikos.*" In *Theological Dictionary of the New Testament*. Edited by Gerhard Friedrich, vol. 5, 841–53. Translated by Geoffrey W. Bromiley. Grand Rapids: Eerdmans, 1967.

Wilbanks, Dana W. *Re-creating America: The Ethics of U.S. Immigration and Refugee Policy in a Christian Perspective*. Nashville: Abingdon, 1996.

Hispanic (Latino/a) Theology

Publications

Aponte, Edwin David, and Miguel A. de la Torre, eds. *Handbook of Latino/a Theologies*. St. Louis: Chalice, 2006.

Badillo, David A. *Latinos and the New Immigrant Church*. Baltimore: Johns Hopkins University Press, 2006.

Carroll R., M. Daniel. "The Bible, the Church, and Human Rights in Contemporary Debates about Hispanic Immigration in the United States." *Journal of Latin American Theology* 2, no. 1 (2007): 161–84.

Costas, Orlando. *Christ beyond the Gate: Mission beyond Christendom*. Maryknoll, NY: Orbis, 1982.

Crespo, Orlando. *Being Latino in Christ: Finding Wholeness in Your Ethnic Identity*. Downers Grove, IL: InterVarsity, 2003.

Elizondo, Virgilio P. *Galilean Journey: The Mexican-American Promise*. Maryknoll, NY: Orbis, 1983.

Escobar, Samuel. "Immigration: Avenue and Challenge to Mission." *Journal of Latin American Theology* 1, no. 2 (2006): 70–94.

Espín, Orlando O. *The Faith of the People: Theological Reflections on Popular Catholicism*. Maryknoll, NY: Orbis, 1997.

Goizueta, Roberto, and Eldin Villafañe, eds. *Hispanic Christian Thought at the Dawn of the 21st Century: Apuntes in Honor of Justo L. Gonzalez*. Nashville: Abingdon, 2005.

González, Justo L. *Mañana: Christian Theology from a Hispanic Perspective*. Nashville: Abingdon, 1990.

———. *Santa Biblia: The Bible through Hispanic Eyes*. Nashville: Abingdon, 1996.

Isasi-Díaz, Ada María, and Fernando F. Segovia, eds. *Hispanic/Latino Theology: Challenge and Promise*. Minneapolis: Fortress, 1996.

Maldonado, David, Jr., ed. *Protestantes/Protestants: Hispanic Christianity within Mainline Traditions*. Nashville: Abingdon, 1999.

Pedraja, Luis G. *Teología: An Introduction to Hispanic Theology*. Nashville: Abingdon, 2003.

Recinos, Harold J. *Good News from the Barrio: Prophetic Witness for the Church*. Louisville: Westminster John Knox, 2006.

Rivera, Luis. "Toward a Diaspora Hermeneutics (Hispanic North America)." In *Character Ethics and the Old Testament: Moral Dimensions of Scripture*, edited by M. Daniel Carroll R. and Jacqueline Lapsley, 169–89. Louisville: Westminster John Knox, 2007.

Rodríguez, José David, and Loida I. Martell-Otero, eds. *Teología En Conjunto: A Collaborative Hispanic Protestant Theology*. Louisville: Westminster John Knox, 1997.

Sánchez-Walsh, Arlene M. *Latino Pentecostal Identity: Evangelical Faith, Self, and Society*. New York: Columbia University Press, 2003.

Soliván, Samuel. *Spirit, Pathos, and Liberation: Toward an Hispanic Pentecostal Theology*. Journal of Pentecostal Theology Supplements Series 14. Sheffield: Sheffield Academic Press, 1998.

Journals

Apuntes

Journal of Hispanic/Latino Theology

Journal of Latin American Theology: Christian Reflections from the Latino South

Perspectivas: Occasional Papers

Internet Sites

US Government

US Census Bureau: www.census.gov/pubinfo/www/NEWhisp ML1.html

US Citizenship and Immigration Services: www.uscis.gov/portal/ site/uscis; www.immigration.gov

US Department of Homeland Security: www.dhs.gov/index .shtm

Sympathetic to Hispanic Immigration

Activist Organizations

BorderLinks: www.BorderLinks.org/bl/index.htm

Immigrant Solidarity Network: www.immigrantsolidarity.org

League of United Latin American Citizens: www.lulac.org

Mexican American Legal Defense and Education Fund: www .maldef.org

Movimiento Estudiantil Chicano de Aztlán: www.nationalme cha.org

National Council of La Raza: www.nclr.org

National Immigration Forum: www.immigrationforum.org

National Network for Immigration and Refugee Rights: www
.nnirr.org

No More Deaths: www.nomoredeaths.org

Think Tanks and Research Centers[1]

Coalition for Comprehensive Immigration Reform: www.cirnow
.org

Immigration Legal Resource Center: www.ilrc.org

Mexican Migration Project: http://mmp.opr.princeton.edu

Migration Policy Institute: www.migrationpolicy.org

Pew Hispanic Center: http://pewhispanic.org

Urban Institute: www.urban.org/immigrants

Opposed to Hispanic Immigration

Activist Organizations

Americans for Immigration Control: www.immigrationcontrol
.com

Americans for Legal Immigration: www.alipac.us/index.php

Immigration's Human Cost: www.immigrationshumancost.org

Minutemen Civil Defense Corps: www.minutemanhq.com

The Minuteman Project: www.minutemanproject.com/mmp

US Border Control: www.usbc.org

Think Tanks and Research Centers

Center for Immigration Studies: www.cis.org

Federation for American Immigration Reform: www.fairus.org/
site/PageServer

Heritage Foundation: www.heritage.org/research/immigration

Immigration Reform Law Institute: www.irli.org

Sierrans for US Population Stabilization: www.susps.org

Religious Organizations

American Baptist Churches: www.faithandpolicy.org/blog/?p=420

Christian Coalition of America: www.cc.org/content.cfm?srch=immigration

Christians for Comprehensive Immigration Reform: www.sojo.net/index.cfm?action=action.display&item=CCIR_main

Church World Service: www.churchworldservice.org/Immigration/index.html

Eagle Forum: www.eagleforum.org

Esperanza USA: www.esperanza.us/site/pp.asp?c=6nJGLONiGiF&b=237530

Evangelical Free Church: www.wheaton.edu/CACE/resources/onlinearticles/immigration.pdf

Evangelical Lutheran Church in America: www.lutheranstateadvocacy.org/socialstatements/immigration

Interfaith Statement in Support of Comprehensive Immigration Reform: www.wr.org/whatwedo/immigrantservices/reform.asp

Lutheran Church–Missouri Synod: www.lcms.org/pages/internal.asp?NavID=10023

Lutheran Immigration and Refugee Service: www.lirs.org/DonateServe/advocate/CIR/OnTheIssue-CIR.pdf

National Association of Evangelicals: www.nae.net/images/Resolution%20on%20Immigration%20%20October%202006.pdf

National Council of Christian Churches: www.churchworldservice.org/Immigration

National Hispanic Christian Leadership Conference: www.nhclc.org

Presbyterian Church (USA): www.pcusa.org/immigration

Reformed Church of America: www.rca.org/NETCOMMUNITY/Page.aspx?&pid=504&srcid=491

Sojourners Community: www.sojo.net/index.cfm?action=resources.discussion_guides

Southern Baptist Convention:
www.sbc.net/resolutions/amResolution.asp?ID=1157

SBC Ethics and Religious Liberty Commission: http://erlc.com/topics/C55

United Methodist Church: www.archives.umc.org/interior_print
.asp?ptid=4&mid=1063

United States Catholic Church:

Catholic Campaign for Immigration Reform: www.justicefor
immigrants.org

Catholic Legal Immigration Network, Inc.: www.cliniclegal
.org

Conference of Catholic Bishops: www.usccb.org/mrs/index
.shtml

"Strangers No Longer: Together on the Journey of Hope":
www.nccbuscc.org/mrs/stranger.htm

Professional Scholarly Associations

ACTHUS: Academy of Catholic Theologians of the United States
(www.acthus.org)

AETH: Asociación para la Educación Teológica Hispana
(www.aeth.org)

HTI: Hispanic Theological Initiative (www.htiprogram.org)

NOTES

Introduction

1. For the impact of the war, see Proyecto Interdiocesano Recuperación de la Memoria Histórica/Catholic Institute for International Relations, *Guatemala: Never Again* (Maryknoll, NY: Orbis, 1999).

2. For government documents, including attempts to respond to complaints about the category "Hispanic," see www.census.gov/popu lation/www/documentation/twps0056.html; www.census.gov/popu lation/www/socdemo/compraceho.html; www.whitehouse.gov/omb/ fedreg/1997standards.html. A collection of reports that demonstrates the interplay of differences and commonalities is Jorge Ramos, *The Other Face of America: Chronicles of the Immigrants Shaping Our Future*, trans. P. J. Duncan (New York: Rayo, 2002).

The choice of an appropriate label is also discussed among Hispanic theologians. See, for example, Fernando F. Segovia, "Aliens in the Promised Land: The Manifest Destiny of U.S. Hispanic American Theology," in *Hispanic/Latino Theology: Challenge and Promise*, ed. Ada María Isasi-Díaz and Fernando F. Segovia (Minneapolis: Fortress, 1996), 15–42 (see esp. 31–42).

3. Another term is "Chicano" (feminine "Chicana"). This word is limited to those of Mexican descent and usually is associated with a more militant approach to Mexican-American ethnicity.

4. Still another category is the "internally displaced." This category includes those who flee from an area of conflict but remain within the boundaries of their country.

Chapter 1: Hispanic Immigration

1. Jorge Ramos, *Dying to Cross: The Worst Immigrant Tragedy in American History*, trans. K. Cordero (New York: Rayo, 2005). The driver, Tyrone Williams, was convicted in January 2007 of fifty-eight counts of conspiracy and of harboring and transporting immigrants. He was sentenced to life without parole. Ironically, Williams is an immigrant from Jamaica.

2. "The Death of Lance Corporal Gutiérrez," CBS News, April 23, 2003, www.cbsnews.com/stories/2003/04/23/60II/main550779.shtml; "Chapín, el primer muerto en batalla," *Siglo xxi*, March 23, 2003, http://old.sigloxxi.com/detallesnews_otraedicion.asp?pag=mcweua01.txt; "Soñaba con ser un gran arquitecto," *Siglo xxi*, March 26, 2003, http://old.sigloxxi.com/detallesnews_otraedicion.asp?pag=mczeua01.txt.

3. For example, Rubén Martínez, *Crossing Over: A Mexican Family on the Migrant Trail* (New York: Metropolitan Books, 2001); Luis Alberto Urrea, *The Devil's Highway: A True Story* (New York: Back Bay Books, 2004). Documented studies of deaths include Karl Eschbach, Jacqueline Hagan, and Nestor Rodríguez, "Deaths during Undocumented Immigration: Trends and Policy Implications in the New Era of Homeland Security," www.uh.edu/cir/Deaths_during_migration.pdf; Raquel Rubio-Goldsmith et al., "A Humanitarian Crisis at the Border: New Estimates of Deaths among Unauthorized Immigrants," www.ailf.org/ipc/policybrief/poli cybrief_020607.shtml. Humanitarian organizations, such as No More Deaths, work to alleviate the hardships of immigrants in the desert. Mention should also be made of the sanctuary movement, a coalition of churches that works to support those immigrants and their families who are targeted for deportation under present immigration law.

4. A Web site dedicated to gathering such accounts in order to stop Hispanic immigration is http://immigrationshumancost.org.

5. Gordon H. Hanson, *Why Does Immigration Divide America? Public Finance and Political Opposition to Open Borders* (Washington, DC: Institute for International Economics, 2005), 41–53. Gia Elise Barboza, Roger Knight, and Timothy Ready, "What Do Black and White Residents of Metropolitan Chicago Think about Latin American and Mexican Immigrants? Findings from the Chicago-Area Survey," *Latino Research@ND* 4, no. 6 (2007). For periodically updated data, see the Gallup Poll at www.galluppoll.com/content/default.aspx?ci=1660.

6. "2006 National Survey of Latinos: The Immigration Debate," Pew Hispanic Center, July 13, 2006, http://pewhispanic.org/files/re ports/68.pdf; "The Latino Electorate: An Analysis of the 2006 Election," Pew Hispanic Center, July 24, 2007, http://pewhispanic.org/files/fact sheets/34.pdf; Ruth Milkman, "Critical Mass: Latino Labor and Politics in California," *NACLA Report on the Americas* 40, no. 3 (2007): 30–36;

Timothy Ready and Roger Knight, "Variations in Political Involvement and Attitudes among Latinos by Birth and Citizenship: Findings from the Chicago-Area Survey," *Latino Research@ND* 4, no. 3 (2007); cf. Ilan Stavans, *Latino History and Culture* (New York: HarperCollins, 2007), 139–51. Immigrant organizations also are lobbying their home governments to bring pressure to bear on the US Congress. For example, in the summer of 2007, CONGUATE (Coalición de Inmigrantes Guatemaltecos en Estados Unidos) met with the leaders of various political parties in Guatemala in the run-up to that country's September 2007 election to ask about their plans to help the Guatemalans in the US, who now number over a million.

7. For a survey of theories, see Douglas S. Massey, Jorge Durand, and Nolan J. Malone, *Beyond Smoke and Mirrors: Mexican Immigration in an Era of Economic Integration* (New York: Russell Sage Foundation, 2002), 9–21. They discuss the models of neoclassic economics, the new economics of labor migration, segmented labor market theory, and the idea of a cumulative causation of migration. A more recent source is Caroline B. Brettell and James F. Hollifield, eds., *Migration Theory: Talking across Disciplines*, 2nd ed. (New York: Routledge, 2008).

8. Recent extensive histories of US immigration are Timothy J. Hatton and Jeffrey G. Williamson, *Global Migration and the World Economy: Two Centuries of Policy and Performance* (Cambridge, MA: MIT Press, 2005); Aristide R. Zohlberg, *A Nation by Design: Immigration Policy in the Fashioning of America* (New York: Russell Sage Foundation; Cambridge, MA: Harvard University Press, 2007). Also see John Higham, *Strangers in the Land: Patterns of American Nativism 1860–1925*, rev. ed. (New Brunswick, NJ: Rutgers University Press, 2002).

9. In addition to Hatton and Williamson, *Global Migration*; Zohlberg, *Nation by Design*; Higham, *Strangers in the Land*; see especially Jean Pfaelzer, *Driven Out: The Forgotten War against Chinese Americans* (New York: Random House, 2007).

10. Massey, Durand, and Malone, *Beyond Smoke and Mirrors*; Joseph Nevins, *Operation Gatekeeper: The Rise of the "Illegal Alien" and the Remaking of the U.S.-Mexico Boundary* (New York: Routledge, 2001); cf. the relevant sections in Hatton and Williamson, *Global Migration*; Zohlberg, *Nation by Design*; Higham, *Strangers in the Land*.

11. The area that is now Arizona and New Mexico was completed with the Gadsden Purchase in December 1853. An excellent, and very readable, recent account of this war is Timothy J. Henderson, *A Glorious Defeat: Mexico and Its War with the United States* (New York: Hill & Wang, 2007). This book presents the buildup to the war and its execution and

aftermath from the Mexican sources. Henderson also comments on how that war has affected Mexican-US relations since that time.

12. The Chicano labor leader César Chávez was prominent at this time. He organized migrant workers in California, who were predominantly Mexican-American, and was instrumental in the creation of the United Farm Workers union (UFW). Some of the activities of the UFW were aimed at eliminating competition for jobs caused by undocumented workers and preventing undocumented workers from being hired as strike-breakers. The years 1965 to 1975 were the high point of Chicano activism.

13. See especially Nevins, *Operation Gatekeeper.*

14. "Enforcing Immigration Law: The Role of State and Local Law Enforcement," Congressional Research Service, August 14, 2006, http://trac.syr.edu/immigration/library/P1072.pdf. The Congressional Research Service is the public policy research arm of the US Congress.

15. "Pennsylvania Town Enacts Strict Illegal Immigration Ordinance," FoxNews.com, July 14, 2006, www.foxnews.com/story/0,2933,203513,00 .html; "Judge Strikes Down Town's Immigration Law," *New York Times,* July 26, 2007, www.nytimes.com/2007/07/26/us/26cnd-hazleton .html?hp.

16. "The Hispanic Population 2000: Census 2000 Brief," www.cen sus.gov/prod/2001pubs/c2kbr01-3.pdf; Jeffrey S. Passel "Unauthorized Migrants: Numbers and Characteristics. Background Briefing Prepared for Task Force on Immigration and America's Future," Pew Hispanic Center, June 14, 2005, http://pewhispanic.org/files/reports/46.pdf; "Fact Sheet: Indicators of Recent Migration Flows from Mexico," Pew Hispanic Center, May 30, 2007, http://pewhispanic.org/factsheets/factsheet .php?FactsheetID=33; "A Statistical Portrait of Hispanics at Mid-Decade," http://pewhispanic.org/reports/middecade.

17. Because Puerto Rico is a commonwealth of the United States, Puerto Ricans are sometimes categorized differently than the Hispanic population that has its roots in the rest of Latin America.

18. This higher birthrate among Hispanics includes those who are immigrants and those who are native born. In both cases, the birthrate is higher than any other ethnic group. See the sources in note 16.

19. Samuel P. Huntington, *The Clash of Civilizations and the Remaking of the World Order* (New York: Simon & Schuster, 1996). His new book is *Who Are We? The Challenges to America's National Identity* (New York: Simon & Schuster, 2004).

20. The most extreme, of course, are the border vigilante groups and white supremacy organizations. See Solana Larsen, "The Anti-Immigration Movement: From Shovels to Suits," *NACLA Report on the Americas* 40, no. 3 (2007): 14–18.

21. Victor Davis Hanson, *Mexifornia: A State of Becoming* (San Francisco: Encounter Books, 2003); Tom Tancredo, *In Mortal Danger: The Battle for America's Border and Security* (Nashville: WND Books, 2006); Patrick J. Buchanan, *State of Emergency: The Third World Invasion and Conquest of America* (New York: Thomas Dunne, 2006).

22. Linda Chávez, *Out of the Barrio: Toward a New Politics of Hispanic Assimilation* (New York: Basic Books, 1991); Chávez, "Our Hispanic Predicament," *Commentary* 105, no. 6 (1998): 47–50. An essay that generated intense reactions is "Latino Fear and Loathing," www.creators.com/opinion/linda-chavez/latino-fear-and-loathing.html; her response to the negative feedback is "Latino Fear and Loathing, Part II," www.creators.com/opininion/linda-chavez/fear-and-loathing-part-ii.html.

23. Richard Rodríguez, *Hunger of Memory: The Education of Richard Rodriguez* (New York: Bantam, 1983); *Days of Obligation: An Argument with My Mexican Father* (New York: Penguin, 1993); *Brown: The Last Discovery of America* (New York: Penguin, 2002). An example of his biting critique of the concept is his chapter "Hispanic" in *Brown*, 103–23.

24. Rainer Muenz, "Europe: Population and Migration in 2005," Migration Policy Institute, June 1, 2006, www.migrationinformation.org/Feature/print.cfm?ID=402; Beatriz Padilla and João Peixoto, "Latin American Migration to Southern Europe," Migration Policy Institute, June 29, 2007, www.migrationinformation.org/Feature/print.cfm?ID=609.

25. Emilio José Gómez Ciriano and Nicole Fuchs, *Inmigrante y ciudadano: Hacia una nueva cultura de la acogida* (Madrid: PPC, 2005). Also note Miguel A. Palomino, "Latino Immigration in Europe: Challenge and Opportunity for Mission," *International Bulletin for Mission Research* 28, no. 2 (2004): 55–58.

26. I am using the term "assimilation" in a loose sense. For a helpful summary of the multiple ways in which immigration communities live in a new land, see Luis Rivera, "Toward a Diaspora Hermeneutics (Hispanic North America)," in *Character Ethics and the Old Testament: Moral Dimensions of Scripture*, ed. M. Daniel Carroll R. and Jacqueline Lapsley (Louisville: Westminster John Knox, 2007), 169–89 (see esp. 172–76).

27. Alejandro Portes and Rubén G. Rumbaut, *Immigrant America: A Portrait*, 3rd ed. (Berkeley: University of California Press, 2006). Anthropological studies are particularly helpful here (I am indebted to David Stoll for directing me to the following sources). See Ann Miles, *From Cuenca to Queens: An Anthropological Story of Transnational Migration* (Austin: University of Texas Press, 2004); Jeffrey H. Cohen, *The Culture of Migration in Southern Mexico* (Austin: University of Texas Press, 2004); Robert Courtney Smith, *Mexican New York: Transnational Lives of New Immigrants* (Berkeley: University of California Press, 2006). A significant element

of identity affected by transnationalism is the concept of citizenship. Concern about citizenship appears in the books by Huntington, Tancredo, and Buchanan. It is addressed by Miles, Cohen, and Smith; note especially Portes and Rumbaut, *Immigrant America*, 117–67. The impact of economic globalization on the nation-state and citizenship is a topic of research, too, as anyone who has read the literature on globalization is aware. International politics also plays a role. Several Latin American countries now allow dual citizenship and permit immigrants to vote in elections. Governments also now try to provide services to émigrés. The Foreign Ministry of Guatemala, for instance, has an arm called the Portal del Migrante dedicated to these issues (www.minex.gob.gt). Membership within a society vis-à-vis outsiders is discussed in legal ethics as well. See, for example, Michael Waltzer, *Spheres of Justice: A Defense of Pluralism and Equality* (New York: Basic Books, 1983), 31–63; William James Booth, "Foreigners: Insiders, Outsiders, and the Ethics of Membership," *Review of Politics* 59, no. 2 (1997): 259–92; William R. O'Neill and William C. Spohn, "Rights of Passage: The Ethics of Immigration and Refugee Policy," *Theological Studies* 59, no. 1 (1998): 84–106. This book is not designed to engage these complex issues, but it is important that the reader be aware of their relevance to the topic at hand.

28. In addition to the sources cited in the previous note, see Sonya Tafoya, "Shades of Belonging," Pew Hispanic Center, December 6, 2004, http://pewhispanic.org/files/reports/35.pdf; Jack Citrin et al., "Testing Huntington: Is Hispanic Immigration a Threat to American Identity?" *Perspectives on Politics* 5, no. 1 (2007): 31–48; Roger Waldinger, "Between Here and There: How Attached Are Latinos to Their Native Country?" Pew Hispanic Center, October 25, 2007, http://pewhispanic.org/reports/report.php?ReportID=80. Note the helpful ethnic identity/assimilation grids in Orlando Crespo, *Being Latino in Christ: Finding Wholeness in Your Ethnic Identity* (Downers Grove, IL: InterVarsity, 2003), 40–53; and John S. Leonard, "The Church in between Cultures: Rethinking the Church in Light of Globalization and Immigration," *Evangelical Missions Quarterly* 40, no. 1 (2004): 62–70.

29. There are many other writers, of course, but here are those I have read: Francisco Goldman, *The Long Night of White Chickens* (New York: Atlantic Monthly, 1992); Goldman, *The Ordinary Seaman* (New York: Atlantic Monthly, 1997); Sandra Cisneros, *Caramelo or Puro Cuento* (New York: Vintage, 2002); Victor Villaseñor, *Burro Genius: A Memoir* (New York: HarperCollins, 2004); Edmundo Paz Soldán, *The Matter of Desire*, trans. Lisa Carter (Boston: Houghton Mifflin, 2001); Julia Álvarez, *How the García Girls Lost Their Accent* (New York: Plume, 1992); Álvarez, *Once upon a Quinceañera: Coming of Age in the U.S.A.* (New York: Viking, 2007).

Cf. Ilan Stavans, *The Hispanic Condition: Reflections on Culture and Identity in America* (New York: HarperCollins, 1995); Mark Griffin and Theron Walker, *Living on the Borders: What the Church Can Learn from Ethnic Immigrant Cultures* (Grand Rapids: Brazos, 2004).

30. Cisneros, *Caramelo or Puro Cuento*, 434.

31. Issues of identity and *mestizaje* have been a source of theological reflection among Hispanic theologians as well, but that discussion is reserved for the next chapter. Another term that should be mentioned is *mulatez*. It refers to the cultural mix with the African (a *mulato* is a dark-skinned person). For simplicity's sake, I will limit myself to *mestizaje*.

32. See the comments of Carlos Fuentes, *The Buried Mirror: Reflections on Spain and the New World* (London: André Deutsch, 1992), 341–55.

33. Huntington prefers the metaphor of tomato soup, in which new elements are added, "enriching the taste, but not significantly altering the substance" (*Who Are We?* 184). A richer appreciation of the melting-pot idea, more optimistic and celebratory of difference, is found in Michael Barone, *The New Americans: How the Melting Pot Can Work Again* (Washington, DC: Regnery, 2001).

34. Tancredo, *In Mortal Danger*, 155–72.

35. "Migrant remittances from the United States to Latin America to reach $45 billion in 2006, says IDB," Inter-American Development Bank, October 18, 2006, www.iadb.org/NEWS/articledetail .cfm?artid=3348&language=En.

36. A sampling: Andrew Sun, Paul Harrington, and Ishwar Khatiwada, "The Impact of New Immigrants on Young Native-Born Workers, 2000–2005," Center for Immigration Studies, September 2006, www .cis.org/articles/2006/back806.html; "Immigration and Rising Income Inequality," Federation for American Immigration Reform, March 2007, www.fairus.org/site/DocServer/Ineqstudy.pdf?docID=1401; Robert Rector, "White House Report Hides the Real Costs of Amnesty and Low Skill Immigration," Heritage Foundation, June 26, 2007, www.heritage.org/ Research/Immigration/upload/wm_1523.pdf.

37. See Hanson, *Why Does Immigration Divide America?* 27–40.

38. For example, Hanson, *Why Does Immigration Divide America?*; George J. Borjas, ed., *Mexican Immigration to the United States*, National Bureau of Economic Research Conference Report (Chicago: University of Chicago Press, 2007).

39. Walter A. Ewing, "Dollars without Sense: Underestimating the Value of Less-Educated Workers," www.ailf.org/ipc/policybrief/policy brief_051807.pdf; Rubén G. Rumbaut and Walter A. Ewing, "The Myth of Immigrant Criminality and the Paradox of Assimilation: Incarceration Rates among Native and Foreign-Born Men," Immigration Policy

Center, Spring 2007, www.ailf.org/ipc/special_report/sr_022107.pdf; Lant Pritchett, *Let Their People Come: Breaking the Gridlock on Global Mobility* (Washington, DC: Center for Global Development, 2006); cf. Portes and Rumbaut, *Immigrant America.*

40. Silvia Irene Palma, ed., *Después de Nuestro Señor, Estados Unidos: Perspectivas de análisis del comportamiento e implicaciones de la migración internacional en Guatemala* (Guatemala: FLACSO, 2004); David Stoll, "El debate migratorio en los Estados Unidos como contienda entre cuatro distintas versiones del sueño norteamericano," presented at the monthly meeting of La Sociedad Evangélica de Estudios Socio-religiosos, Guatemala City, July 4, 2007. Note the difference in tone between the optimism of a 2004 report ("Aporte de migrantes en EE.UU. trae prosperidad," *Prensa Libre,* July 4, 2004, http://prensalibre.com/pl/2004/julio/04/92208 .html) and the more pessimistic view in 2007 ("El fantasma del sueño americano," *Prensa Libre,* February 5, 2007, http://prensalibre.com/ pl/2007/febrero/05/162660.html; "Ingreso de remesas registra caída," *Siglo xxi,* July 6, 2007, http://sigloxxi.com/index.php?link=noticias& noticiaid=12639). My example is Guatemala, but there is research on other places, such as Cuenca, Bolivia (Miles, *From Cuenca to Queens*), and Oaxaca, Mexico (Smith, *Mexican New York*; Cohen, *Culture of Migration in Southern Mexico*; Leah K. VanWey, Catherine M. Tucker, and Eileen Diaz McConnell, "Community Organization, Migration, and Remittances in Oaxaca," *Latin American Research Review* 40, no. 1 [2005]: 83–107).

41. For economic globalization and the migration of labor (although these sources do not all take the same point of view), see Pritchett, *Let Their People Come*; Jagdish Bhagwati, *In Defense of Globalization* (New York: Oxford University Press, 2004); Joseph E. Stiglitz and Andrew Charlton, *Fair Trade for All: How Trade Can Promote Development* (New York: Oxford University Press, 2005); Brettell and Hollifield, *Migration Theory*; cf. M. Daniel Carroll R., "The Challenge of Economic Globalization for Theology: From Latin America to a Hermeneutics of Responsibility," in *Globalizing Theology: Christian Belief and Practice in an Era of World Christianity,* ed. C. Ott and H. Netland (Grand Rapids: Baker Academic, 2006), 199–212.

42. It is interesting to look at Thomas L. Friedman's analysis of Mexico in the new global market in his best-selling *The World Is Flat: A Brief History of the Twenty-First Century* (New York: Farrar, Straus and Giroux, 2005), 309–36. He speaks of government bureaucracy, cultural patterns, and the imperative to change its vision and ways of operating its economy, but nowhere does he mention the human cost or labor migration as consequences of Mexico's situation. For a spirited defense of Mexico's journey into the global economy, see Vicente Fox with Rob

Allyn, *Revolution of Hope: The Life, Faith, and Dreams of a Mexican President* (New York: Viking, 2007).

43. Portes and Rumbaut, "Religion," chap. 9 in *Immigrant America*, 299–342; "Changing Faiths: Latinos and the Transformation of American Religion," Pew Hispanic Center, April 25, 2007, http://pewhispanic .org/reports/report.php?ReportID=75. Also note David Maldonado, ed., *Protestantes/Protestants: Hispanic Christianity within Mainline Traditions* (Nashville: Abingdon, 1999); Juan F. Martínez Guerra and Luis Scott, eds., *Iglesias peregrinas en busca de identidad: Cuadros del protestantismo latino en los Estados Unidos* (Buenos Aires, Argentina: Kairós, 2004); Edwin I. Hernández, Milagros Peña, Kenneth Davis, and Elizabeth Station, *Strengthening Hispanic Ministry across Denominations: A Call to Action*, Pulpit and Pew: Research on Pastoral Leadership (Durham, NC: Duke Divinity School, 2005); the pertinent chapters in Edwin David Aponte and Miguel A. de la Torre, eds., *Handbook of Latino/a Theologies* (St. Louis: Chalice, 2006).

44. Virgilio Elizondo, *Galilean Journey: The Mexican-American Promise* (Maryknoll, NY: Orbis, 1983), 32–48; Orlando O. Espín, *The Faith of the People: Theological Reflections on Popular Catholicism* (Maryknoll, NY: Orbis, 1997); the pertinent chapters in Aponte and de la Torre, *Handbook of Latino/a Theologies*; David A. Badillo, *Latinos and the New Immigrant Church* (Baltimore: Johns Hopkins University Press, 2006).

45. The amount of literature on Latin American Pentecostalism is huge, and the number of studies on Hispanic Pentecostalism is growing. For helpful introductions, see José Míguez Bonino, *Faces of Latin American Protestantism* (Grand Rapids: Eerdmans, 1997), 53–77; Samuel Solivan, *The Spirit, Pathos and Liberation: Toward an Hispanic Pentecostal Theology*, Journal of Pentecostal Theology Supplements Series 14 (Sheffield: Sheffield Academic Press, 1998); Samuel Escobar, *Changing Tides: Latin America & World Mission Today* (Maryknoll, NY: Orbis, 2002), 77–149; Arlene M. Sánchez Walsh, *Latino Pentecostal Identity: Evangelical Faith, Self, and Society*, Religion and American Culture Series (New York: Columbia University Press, 2003).

46. Gastón Espinosa, Virgilio Elizondo, and Jesse Miranda, *Latino Religions and Civic Activism in the United States* (New York: Oxford University Press, 2005); "Immigrant-Led Organizers in Their Own Voices: Local Realities and Shared Visions," Catholic Legal Immigration Network, May 2006, www.cliniclegal.org/Publications/Freepublications/CLINIC_Repor tonorganizers_final.pdf; cf. Pew Hispanic Center, "Changing Faiths."

47. Note, for example, Griffin and Walker, *Living on the Borders*; Harold J. Recinos, *Good News from the Barrio: Prophetic Witness for the Church* (Louisville: Westminster John Knox, 2006); Samuel Escobar, "Immigration:

Avenue and Challenge to Mission," *Journal of Latin American Theology* 1, no. 2 (2006): 70–94. An older, but important, clarion call is Orlando Costas, *Christ beyond the Gate: Mission beyond Christendom* (Maryknoll, NY: Orbis, 1982). Also note the list of works in the appendix of contributions by Hispanic theologians.

48. Philip Jenkins, *The Next Christendom: The Coming of Global Christianity* (New York: Oxford University Press, 2002). Note the statistics in David B. Barrett, Todd M. Johnson, and Peter F. Crossing, "Missiometrics 2007: Creating Your Own Analysis of Global Data," *International Bulletin of Missionary Research* 31, no. 1 (2007): 25–32; cf. Jehu J. Hanciles, "Migration and Mission: Some Implications for the Twenty-first Century Church," *International Review of Missionary Research* 27, no. 4 (2003): 146–53. In missiological studies, the labels "southern hemisphere" and "global south" are not exact terms. Christian growth has been phenomenal in Latin America, Africa, and southern Asia—all of which lie to the south of Western Europe and the United States and Canada—but it is also evident in Eastern Europe and other parts of Asia (such as China and South Korea).

49. Philip Jenkins, *The New Faces of Christianity: Believing the Bible in the Global South* (New York: Oxford University Press, 2006); cf. Ott and Netland, *Globalizing Theology.*

50. During the era of the Cold War, the label *Third World* referred to those countries not in Western Europe and North America (the First World) or in the Soviet Union (the Second World). The term *Two-Thirds World* arose after the demise of the Soviet Union as a description for the part of the globe that held two-thirds of the planet's population and landmass. Another term that is increasingly used is *Majority World.* Today the labels *Two-Thirds World* and *Majority World* are occasionally applied to ministry groups in Western Europe and the US.

Chapter 2: Of Immigrants, Refugees, and Exiles

1. Scholarly resources are mentioned in the endnotes for those who might desire to pursue details in greater depth. Nevertheless, I have kept these to a minimum because of the more popular focus of this book.

2. There is a huge amount of material by Hispanic scholars regarding the importance of reading the Bible with an explicitly Hispanic lens. This is an important point that I affirm, but the confines of this book do not permit an exploration of that hermeneutical discussion. See the appendix for sources that address this issue and note 22 below. It also is worthwhile to distinguish between what scholars might argue are essential ingredients for a Hispanic approach to the biblical text and the jargon that is utilized in those proposals (such as consciously

reading from "on the border" or from *nepantla*) and what actually goes on among Hispanic laypeople and in Hispanic churches. The focus there often is on personal and familial needs or largely is influenced, for example, by certain Pentecostal themes. Societal issues usually remain in the background, except as they immediately affect church members. The importance of distinguishing the academic discourse of minority or Two-Thirds World groups from that of the "common people" is addressed by Jenkins in *The New Faces of Christianity*.

3. Conferencia del Episcopado Mexicano and the United States Conference of Catholic Bishops, *Strangers No Longer: Together on the Journey of Hope* (Washington, DC: United States Conference of Catholic Bishops, 2003), www.nccbuscc.org/mrs/stranger.htm); cf. William R. O'Neill and William C. Spohn, "Rights of Passage: The Ethics of Immigration and Refugee Policy," *Theological Studies* 59, no. 1 (1998): 84–106; Andrew M. Yuengert, *Inhabiting the Land: The Case for the Right to Migrate*, Christian Social Thought Series 6 (Grand Rapids: Acton Institute, 2003), 11–18. Pope John Paul II's "Migration Day" messages are available on the Vatican Web site (www.vatican.va); for CELAM, visit www.celam.org.

4. For illuminating discussions on the image of God from a missiological perspective, see Christopher J. H. Wright, *Old Testament Ethics for the People of God* (Downers Grove, IL: InterVarsity, 2004), 116–29; Wright, *The Mission of God* (Downers Grove, IL: InterVarsity, 2007), 421–28.

5. O'Neill and Spohn, "Rights of Passage," 91–97; "Convention on the Protection of the Rights of All Migrant Workers and Members of Their Families," UN Office of the High Commission for Human Rights, www.unhchr.ch/html/menu3/b/m_mwctoc.htm; cf. Silvia Irene Palma, ed., *Después de Nuestro Señor, Estados Unidos: Perspectivas de análisis del comportamiento e implicaciones de la migración internacional en Guatemala* (Guatemala: FLACSO, 2004).

6. An important figure in this theological reflection has been Virgilio Elizondo and his book *Galilean Journey: The Mexican-American Promise* (Maryknoll, NY: Orbis, 1983). He compares the racial mix and challenges of the Mexican-American to those of the Galilean Jesus. Also note Fernando F. Segovia, "The Text as Other: Towards a Hispanic American Hermeneutic," in *Text & Experience: Towards a Cultural Exegesis of the Bible*, ed. Daniel Smith-Christopher, Biblical Seminar 35 (Sheffield: Sheffield Academic Press, 1995), 276–98 (see esp. 286–90); Justo L. González, *Santa Biblia: The Bible through Hispanic Eyes* (Nashville: Abingdon, 1996), 77–90; Luis G. Pedraja, *Teología: An Introduction to Hispanic Theology* (Nashville: Abingdon, 2003), 78–80; Orlando Crespo, *Being Latino in Christ: Finding Wholeness in Your Ethnic Identity* (Downers Grove, IL: InterVarsity, 2003); cf. Bob Ekblad, *Reading the Bible with the Damned* (Louisville: Westminster

John Knox, 2005), 21–24. For a popular discussion, see Jesse Miranda, "The Hispanic Man: The Mascot," in *We Stand Together: Reconciling Men of Different Color*, ed. Rod Cooper (Chicago: Moody, 1995), 97–110.

7. Each of the items in this list has pastoral concerns as its root. For example, in terms of family issues: immigrants who have left spouses and children in their home country and have another family or partner in the US, the incidence of alcoholism and drug use, the allure of gangs for young people, the temptation of irresponsible consumerism after coming from a more deprived background.

8. In this book I will use the term "sojourner" instead of another valid translation option, "resident alien." In today's climate, there may be some controversial connotations attached to "resident" and "alien." "Sojourner" is a more neutral label.

9. James K. Hoffmeier, *Israel in Egypt: The Evidence for the Authenticity of the Exodus Tradition* (New York: Oxford University Press, 1996), 52–76.

10. Anthony Leahy, "Ethnic Diversity in Ancient Egypt," in *Civilizations of the Ancient Near East*, ed. Jack M. Sasson, 4 vols. (Peabody, MA: Hendrickson, 1995), 1:225–34; Edda Bresciani, "Foreigners," in *The Egyptians*, ed. S. Donadoni (Chicago: University of Chicago Press, 1997), 221–53; Hoffmeier, *Israel in Egypt*, 77–106; K. A. Kitchen, *On the Reliability of the Old Testament* (Grand Rapids: Eerdmans, 2003), 343–52.

11. Magen Broshi and Israel Finkelstein, "The Population of Palestine in Iron Age II," *Bulletin of the American Schools of Oriental Research* 287 (1992): 47–60; Israel Finkelstein, "The Archaeology of the Days of Manasseh," in *Scripture and Other Artifacts: Essays in Honor of Philip J. King*, ed. M. Coogan et al. (Louisville: John Knox, 1994), 169–87.

12. The text of Sennacherib's account of his third campaign, of which the siege of Jerusalem was a part, is found in *The Context of Scripture*, ed. William H. Hallo, vol. 2, *Monumental Inscriptions from the Biblical World* (Leiden: Brill, 2000), 302–3.

13. Hoffmeier, *Israel in Egypt*, 138–44.

14. Ibid., 109–22.

15. K. Lawson Younger Jr., "'Give Us Our Daily Bread': Everyday Life for the Israelite Deportees," in *Life and Culture in the Ancient Near East*, ed. R. E. Averbeck, M. W. Chavalas, and D. B. Weisberg (Bethesda, MD: CDL Press, 2003), 269–88; Bustaney Oded, *Mass Deportations and Deportees in the Neo-Assyrian Empire* (Weisbaden: Dr. Ludwig Reichert Verlag, 1979), 75–115; various articles in K. Van Lerberghe and A. Schoors, eds., *Immigration and Emigration within the Ancient Near East: Festschrift E. Lipiński*, Orientalia Lovaniensia Analecta 65 (Leuven: Uitgeverij Peeters en Departement Oriëntalistiek, 1995).

16. In addition to the biblical text, note Laurie E. Pearce, "New Evidence for Judeans in Babylonia," in *Judah and the Judeans in the Persian Period*, ed. Oded Lipschits and Manfred Oeming (Winona Lake, IN: Eisenbrauns, 2006), 399–411. Also see the sources in the preceding note.

17. Daniel L. Smith has applied refugee and trauma studies to the Exile in *The Religion of the Landless: The Social Context of the Exile* (Bloomington, IN: Meyer-Stone, 1989), and *A Biblical Theology of Exile* (Minneapolis: Fortress, 2002). People in these situations demonstrate several characteristics listed in this paragraph.

18. A topic of contemporary debate among scholars who specialize in the postexilic period is the possible conflict between the returnees and those who had remained in the Land. They suggest that there could have been controversy over, for example, who had the right to the sociopolitical and religious leadership of the new community. Concerns like these may have motivated the writers of Ezra and Nehemiah to include genealogies (though some argue that these are fictitious and were created in self-interest).

19. For these and other issues, see Karen Jobes, *Esther*, New Application Commentary (Grand Rapid: Zondervan, 1999). For more details on the gate and women in the palace, see Pierre Briant, *From Cyrus to Alexander: A History of the Persian Empire*, trans. P. T. Daniels (Winona Lake, IN: Eisenbrauns, 2002), 259–61 and 277–86, respectively.

20. Esther is the only book of the Bible that does not mention God. This caused some ancients to doubt whether it should be included in the canon. The Septuagint, which is the Greek translation of the Hebrew text, resolved the problem by adding over one hundred lines to the book. The additions include prayers and the insertion of the name of God.

21. Jacob Neusner, "Babylonia," *Encyclopaedia Judaica*, 2nd ed. (Detroit: Macmillan, 2007), 3:24–30; Nissim Kazzaz, "Iraq," *Encyclopaedia Judaica*, 10:14–21.

22. Luis Rivera, "Toward a Diaspora Hermeneutics (Hispanic North America)," in *Character Ethics and the Old Testament: Moral Dimensions of Scripture*, ed. M. Daniel Carroll R. and Jacqueline Lapsley (Louisville: Westminster John Knox, 2007); Segovia, "The Text as Other," 276–98; Segovia, "In the World but Not of It: Exile as a Locus for a Theology of the Diaspora," in Isasi-Díaz and Segovia, *Hispanic/Latino Theology*, 195–217; González, *Santa Biblia*, 91–102; Ada María Isasi-Díaz, "'By the Rivers of Babylon': Exile as a Way of Life," in *Reading from This Place: Social Location and Biblical Interpretation in Global Perspective*, ed. Fernando Segovia and Mary Ann Tolbert (Minneapolis: Fortress, 1995), 149–63; Daniel Castelo, "Resident *and* Legal Aliens," *Apuntes* 23, no. 2 (2003): 65–77; cf. Ekblad, *Reading the Bible with the Damned*, 113–26.

23. This is also the title of a book by Eldin Villafañe, *Seek the Peace of the City: Reflections on Urban Ministry* (Grand Rapids: Eerdmans, 1995).

24. Hans de Wit, *En la dispersión, el texto es patria: Introducción a la hermenéutica clásica, moderna y posmoderna* (San José, Costa Rica: Universidad Bíblica Latinoamericana, 2002).

Chapter 3: The Law and the Sojourner

1. Patrick J. Buchanan, *State of Emergency: The Third World Invasion and Conquest of America* (New York: Thomas Dunne, 2006), 220–25.

2. Philip J. King and Lawrence E. Stager, *Life in Biblical Israel*, Library of Ancient Israel (Louisville: Westminster John Knox, 2001), 61–63; cf. Victor H. Matthews and Don C. Benjamin, *Social World of Ancient Israel, 1250–587 BCE* (Peabody, MA: Hendrickson, 1993), 82–95; Andrew Arterbury, *Entertaining Angels: Early Christian Hospitality in Its Mediterranean Setting*, New Testament Monographs 8 (Sheffield: Sheffield Phoenix Press, 2005), 55–93, and passim.

3. Christopher J. H. Wright, *Old Testament Ethics for the People of God* (Downers Grove, IL: InterVarsity, 2004), 68. His full discussion appears on pages 48–75, 182–211. For Deut. 4:5–8, see *Mission of God*, 378–80.

4. One debate among scholars who study Old Testament law is whether the shared vocabulary and ideas of these law codes suggests that they stem from a shared Mesopotamian legal tradition.

5. Moshe Weinfeld, *Social Justice in Ancient Israel and in the Ancient Near East* (Minneapolis: Fortress; Jerusalem: Magnes, 1995); J. Gordon McConville, *God and Earthly Power: An Old Testament Political Theology, Genesis-Kings*, Library of Hebrew Bible/Old Testament Studies 454 (London: T&T Clark, 2007); cf. Peter T. Vogt, *Deuteronomic Theology and the Significance of Torah: A Reappraisal* (Winona Lake, IN: Eisenbrauns, 2006).

6. The key figure here is Clifford Geertz. Note his "Local Knowledge: Fact and Law in Comparative Perspective," in Geertz, *Local Knowledge: Further Essays in Interpretive Anthropology* (New York: Basic Books, 1983), 167–234; and "Off Echoes: Some Comments on Anthropology and Law," *Political and Legal Anthropology Review* 19, no. 2 (1996): 33–37.

7. D. I. Block, "Sojourner," *International Standard Bible Encyclopaedia*, ed. G. W. Bromiley, rev. ed. (Grand Rapids: Eerdmans, 1988), 4:561–64; D. Kellermann, "*gûr*," *Theological Dictionary of the Old Testament*, ed. G. J. Botterweck and H. Ringgren (Grand Rapids: Eerdmans, 1975), 2:439–49; R. J. D. Knauth, "Alien, Foreign Resident," *Dictionary of the Old Testament: Pentateuch*, ed. T. Desmond Alexander and David W. Baker (Downers Grove, IL: InterVarsity, 2003), 26–33; José E. Ramírez Kidd, *Alterity and Identity in Israel: The Ger in the Old Testament*, Beihefte zur Zeitschrift für die alttestamentliche Wissenschaft 283 (Berlin: de Gruyter, 1999).

8. There are exceptions to this generalization, of course. *Zār* can refer to lay Israelites who are not Levites (Exod. 29:13; Lev. 22:10–13; Num. 1:51; 3:10, 38); they are "foreign" in the sense that they are not qualified to do what only the priests can perform.

9. *Nokrî*: other gods (Josh. 24:20), followers of other gods (Ezek. 44:7–9), the licentious woman (Prov. 6:24), or foreign women (1 Kings 11:1; Ezra 10:2; Neh. 13:26). *Zār*: enemies (Ps. 54:3 [54:5 MT]; Isa. 1:7; 29:5), foreign gods (Deut. 32:16; Jer. 2:25), an adulterous woman (Prov. 22:14). These two terms can appear in parallel, referring to, for example, an immoral woman (Prov. 2:16; 5:20; 7:5) or enemies (Obad. 11). They also occur together when they refer to different things "foreign" (Jer. 5:19). These are selected verses. The terms appear in many other passages.

10. In passages such as Prov. 6:1 and 11:15 there is a question whether the "stranger" is an individual who is not well known or a literal foreigner. If the latter, then these passages are a warning not to do business with these foreigners.

11. 1 Chron. 29:15 and Ps. 39:12 [39:13 MT] have this pairing, too, but in reference to the experience of Israelites.

12. The focus here is entirely on the noun *gēr*. It occurs over ninety times in the Old Testament. Its verbal root, *gûr* I, appears eighty-one times and is usually translated as "sojourn" or "live."

13. Even with these distinctions, there is never the negative reaction to *gēr* that one encounters with *nokrî* and *zār*. The clearest example of this difference in response is found in the fact that the passages that condemn intermarriage in Ezra (chaps. 9–10) and Nehemiah (chap. 13) use *nokrî* and *zār*, never *gēr*, to refer to the women rejected by Israel's leaders.

14. Ramírez Kidd, *Alterity and Identity in Israel*, 110–16; cf. the source above in note 15 of chapter 2.

15. For the Laws of Eshnunna and Hammurabi, see Hallo, *Context of Scripture*, 2:332–35 and 335–53, respectively.

16. In addition to the sources in note 7 of this chapter, see R. Rendtorff, "The *Ger* in the Priestly Laws of the Pentateuch," in *Ethnicity and the Bible*, ed. Mark G. Brett, Biblical Interpretation Series (Leiden: Brill, 1996), 77–87; cf. Donald E. Gowan, "Wealth and Poverty in the Old Testament: The Case of the Widow, the Orphan, and the Sojourner," *Interpretation* 41, no. 4 (1987): 341–53; Patrick D. Miller, "Israel as Host to Strangers," in *Israelite Religion and Biblical Theology: Collected Essays*, ed. Patrick D. Miller, Journal for the Study of the Old Testament Supplement Series 267 (Sheffield: Sheffield Academic Press, 2000), 548–71. Many scholars try to construct a history of the development of the responses

to and legislation for the *gēr* based on a reconstruction of the hypothetical history of the production of the law collections in the Pentateuch. Others connect the laws to different historical events, such as the influx of refugees into Judah after the fall of Israel in the late eighth century. I offer a more synchronic presentation of the material.

17. Levites are sometimes included in these measures because in the Law they are not able to own property (Deut. 14:27–29; 16:11, 14; 26:12–13). The verb *gûr* I is applied to them (they "sojourn" in the Land, Deut. 18:6), but the noun *gēr* never is.

18. Exod. 12:19, 49; Lev. 16:29; 17:15; 18:26; 19:34; 24:16, 22; Num. 9:14; 15:29–30; cf. Lev. 19:34; 25:35.

19. For wonderful discussions of foreigners within Israel, see J. Daniel Hays, *From Every People and Nation: A Biblical Theology of Race*, New Studies in Biblical Theology 14 (Leicester: Apollos; Downers Grove, IL: InterVarsity, 2003).

20. *Nokrî* also occurs in Isa. 60:10 and 61:5 (along with *zār*). These passages speak of the judgment on the nations who had cruelly oppressed the people of God. Here, the negative connotation of "foreign" reappears.

21. Another topic to explore, for example, would be ethnicity—how it was understood in the ancient world and throughout history and how it is conceived of today. See D. Block, "Nations, Nationality," *New International Dictionary of Old Testament Theology and Exegesis*, ed. Willem VanGemeren (Grand Rapids: Zondervan, 1997), 4:966–72; K. L. Sparks, "Ethnicity," *Dictionary of the Old Testament: Historical Books*, ed. Bill T. Arnold and H. G. M. Williamson (Downers Grove, IL: InterVarsity, 2005), 268–72.

Chapter 4: Welcoming the Stranger

1. See, for example, Craig A. Evans, *Fabricating Jesus: How Modern Scholars Distort the Gospels* (Downers Grove, IL: InterVarsity, 2006); Richard Bauckham, *Jesus and the Eyewitnesses: The Gospels as Eyewitness Testimony* (Grand Rapids: Eerdmans, 2006).

2. Craig S. Keener, *A Commentary on the Gospel of Matthew* (Grand Rapids: Eerdmans, 1999), 110–11 (see his excursus on the magi on p. 99); cf. Darrell L. Bock and Gregory J. Herrick, *Jesus in Context: Background Readings for Gospel Study* (Grand Rapids: Baker Academic, 2005), 52–54.

3. Craig L. Blomberg, *Jesus and the Gospels: An Introduction and Survey* (Nashville: Broadman & Holman, 1997), 7–71; Ekhard J. Schnabel, *Early Christian Mission*, vol. 1, *Jesus and the Twelve* (Downers Grove, IL: InterVarsity; Leicester: Apollos, 2004), 177–206.

4. K. Haacker, "Samaritan, Samaria," in *The New International Dictionary of New Testament Theology*, ed. Colin Brown (Grand Rapids:

Zondervan, 1975), 3:449–67; H. G. M. Williamson, "Samaritans," in *Dictionary of Jesus and the Gospels*, ed. Joel B. Green, Scott McKnight, and I. Howard Marshall (Downers Grove, IL: InterVarsity, 1992), 724–28; cf. J. Massyngberde Ford, *My Enemy Is My Guest: Jesus and Violence in Luke* (Maryknoll, NY: Orbis, 1984), 80–86.

5. Schnabel, *Early Christian Mission*, 1:242–47, 260–62.

6. D. A. Carson, *The Gospel according to John* (Leicester: Inter-Varsity; Grand Rapids: Eerdmans, 1991), 215–16; Bock and Herrick, *Jesus in Context*, 211–12.

7. Bock and Herrick, *Jesus in Context*, 212.

8. Darrell L. Bock, *Luke, vol. 2*, Baker Exegetical Commentary on the New Testament (Grand Rapids: Baker Academic, 1996), 1405–6.

9. Craig L. Blomberg, *Interpreting the Parables* (Downers Grove, IL: InterVarsity, 1990), 229–33; cf. Bock, *Luke, vol. 2*, 1018–35; Ford, *My Enemy Is My Guest*, 91–94.

10. In terms of the Old Testament, note, for instance: the sheep and goats (Ezek. 34:17), the Son of Man (Dan. 7), coming with the angels (Zech. 14:5). For details, see Keener, *Commentary on the Gospel of Matthew*, 602–4; Bock and Herrick, *Jesus in Context*, 183–85.

11. Ivor H. Jones, *The Matthean Parables: A Literary and Historical Commentary*, Novum Testamentum Supplements 80 (Leiden: Brill, 1995), 246–49; W. D. Davies and Dale C. Allison, *A Critical and Exegetical Commentary on the Gospel of Saint Matthew*, International Critical Commentary (Edinburgh: T&T Clark, 1997), 3:422–23; cf. Ernesto Cardenal, "The Last Judgment (Matt. 25:31–46)," in Ernesto Cardenal, *The Gospel in Solentiname*, trans. Donald D. Walsh (Maryknoll, NY: Orbis, 1982), 4:49–60.

12. For "little ones" and "the least" (the superlative of "little ones"), see 5:19; 10:42; 11:11; 18:6, 10, 14. For "brothers" as disciples, see 5:22–24, 47; 7:3–5; 12:48–50; 18:15, 21, 35; 23:8; 28:10; as Jesus's siblings, see 12:46–47; 13:55; as the siblings of others, see 1:2, 11; 4:18, 21; 10:2, 21; 14:3; 17:1; 19:29; 20:24–25.

13. Craig L. Blomberg, *Matthew*, New American Commentary 22 (Nashville: Broadman & Holman, 1992), 377–80; Keener, *Commentary on the Gospel of Matthew*, 604–6.

14. Note the reflections by Aquiles Ernesto Martínez in "Jesus, the Immigrant Child: A Diasporic Reading of Matthew 2:1–23," *Apuntes* 26, no. 3 (2006): 84–114.

15. In his article "The Least of These My Brothers: Matthew 25:31–46" (*Apuntes* 23, no. 3 [2003]: 100–109), David Cortés-Fuentes despairs that there is no direct correlation to all the needy of the Hispanic community and concludes that they cannot wait for the majority culture to help; they must take the initiative to take care of themselves. I believe that

he has missed the potential application of the passage and the thrust of the Bible in general.

16. Of course, there are many sources one could cite. Of those already cited, see especially Blomberg, *Jesus and the Gospels*, 145–47, 290–91, 388–92; cf. Scot McKnight, *A New Vision for Israel: The Teachings of Jesus in National Context* (Grand Rapids: Eerdmans, 1999), 156–237. It is worth noting that Willard M. Swartley places the Samaritan issue within Jesus's vision of peace and peacemaking in *Covenant of Peace: The Missing Peace in New Testament Theology and Ethics* (Grand Rapids: Eerdmans, 2006), 140–44 (Luke 10), 304–23 (John 4).

17. For this vocabulary in general and how the Septuagint (the Greek translation of the Hebrew text) rendered the Hebrew terminology, see K. L. Schmidt, M. A. Schmidt, and R. Meyer, *"paroikos,"* in *Theological Dictionary of the New Testament*, ed. Gerhard Friedrich, trans. Geoffrey W. Bromiley (Grand Rapids: Eerdmans, 1967), 5:841–53; H. Bietenhard and F. S. Rothenberg, "Foreign, Alien, Dispersion, Stranger," in Brown, *New International Dictionary of New Testament Theology*, 1:683–92. The most extensive discussions are found in John H. Elliott, *A Home for the Homeless: A Sociological Exegesis of 1 Peter, Its Situation and Strategy* (Minneapolis: Fortress, 1990), 21–36; and Elliott, *1 Peter*, Anchor Bible 37B (New York: Doubleday, 2000), 476–83.

18. The NIV actually has "strangers in the world." The phrase "in the world" is not in the Greek text and is an interpretive translation.

19. The former position is argued by Elliott (*Home for the Homeless*, 37–100; *1 Peter*, passim); the latter view by Karen H. Jobes, *1 Peter*, Baker Exegetical Commentary on the New Testament (Grand Rapids: Baker Academic, 2005), 28–42. The social settings of the writer and the recipients are major topics of research on the epistle.

20. Christine D. Pohl has done a lot of work surveying theological themes and the history of the practice, offering practical advice for Christians and churches, and applying this material to refugees and immigration. See her *Making Room: Recovering Hospitality as a Christian Tradition* (Grand Rapids: Eerdmans, 1999); "Biblical Issues in Mission and Migration," *Missiology: An International Review* 31, no. 1 (2003): 3–15; "Responding to Strangers: Insights from the Christian Tradition," *Studies in Christian Ethics* 19, no. 1 (2006): 81–101. For an exegetical approach, see Arterbury, *Entertaining Angels*.

21. In her publications, Pohl also highlights Matt. 25:31–46. This text has been important in reflections on Christian hospitality to all, even if exegetically the biblical text is more focused.

22. Here I am engaging a popular evangelical Christian point of view. I am fully aware that many Christians do not interpret Romans 13 in

such a positive manner. I would sympathize with that less sanguine view. Other passages (and historical experience!) put in doubt an interpretation that holds without much question that the government is always God's instrument for good.

Chapter 5: Where Do We Go from Here?

1. Stanley Hauerwas and William H. Willimon, *Resident Aliens: Life in the Christian Colony. A Provocative Christian Assessment of Culture and Ministry for People Who Know That Something Is Wrong* (Nashville: Abingdon, 1989); cf. Stanley Hauerwas, *In Good Company: The Church as Polis* (Notre Dame: University of Notre Dame Press, 1995).

2. I have applied some of Hauerwas's insights to the immigration debate elsewhere. See M. Daniel Carroll R., "The Bible, the Church, and Human Rights in Contemporary Debates about Hispanic Immigration in the United States," *Journal of Latin American Theology* 2, no. 1 (2007): 161–84.

3. In what follows I am heavily indebted to the profound work of Miroslav Volf, *Exclusion and Embrace: A Theological Exploration of Identity, Otherness, and Reconciliation* (Nashville: Abingdon, 1996). The Serbian-Croatian war motivated his reflections. For his discussion of "soft embrace," see *Exclusion and Embrace*, 140–47.

Appendix

1. A number of universities have immigration research centers. Examples are the University of California–San Diego Center for Comparative Immigration Studies (www.ccis-ucsd.org) and the University of Notre Dame's Institute for Latino Studies (www.nd.edu/~latino). Another source of information is the Chicano and Latino/a departments in universities nationwide.

INDEX

assimilation. *See* Hispanic(s):
    assimilation; migration;
    sojourner: assimilation

bracero program, 34

Christianity
    browning of, 60–62, 163n48,
        163n50
    Hispanic. *See* Hispanic(s):
        Christian presence

Hispanic(s)
    anthropological studies, transna-
        tionalism, 45, 158n27, 159n28
    assimilation, 40–43, 45, 158n26,
        160n33
    Christian presence, 56–59,
        163n48
    identity, 43–44
    impact on American culture,
        17–18, 47–48
    literature, 46–47
    mestizaje, 47, 70, 160n31
    terminology, 21–22, 154nn2–4

theology, 57–59, 163–64n2,
    170–71n15
hospitality
    New Testament, 129–30
    Old Testament, 92–94

image of God, 65–70
immigration
    Bible. *See* Law, Bible; migration
    church statements about, 65
    demographics, 39–40,
        157nn17–18
    economic impact
        costs of, 49
        global migrant labor, 54–55,
            161n42
        international trade, 55
        job market, 49, 51–52, 55,
            157n12
        remittances, 50, 53–54
        Social Security, 52
        social services, 50
    history of
        African, 32
        Chinese, 31

Hispanic, 32–36, 156n11,
157n12
human cost of, 25–27, 155nn1–4
legislation
enforcement, 30, 33, 37–38
laws, 30–37, 54
national identity, 40, 47–48
organizations
advocacy groups, 150–51
opposition groups, 50, 151,
155n4, 157n20
terminology, biblical, 99–101,
122, 126–28, 165n8, 168nn9–
13, 168n16, 169nn17–18,
169n20, 171n17. *See also*
Hispanic(s): terminology

Jesus
encounters with Samaritans,
118–20
as refugee, 115–16
teachings of, 120–23

Law, Bible
ancient Near East, 102, 167n4
anthropological studies, 99
Old Testament
as paradigm, 98, 108
sojourner, 101–7, 109
Romans 13, 131–34, 171n22

migration
Abram, 72–73

Assyria, 78, 81–82
Babylon, 78, 81–83
contemporary. *See* immigration:
economic impact
Daniel, 77–78
deportees, 78
escapees, 79
Egypt, 80–81
Esther, 84, 166n20
Ezra, 83, 166n18
Jesus. *See* Jesus: as refugee
Joseph, 76–77
Moses, 79
Nehemiah, 83, 166n18
patriarchs, 72–74
refugees, 71
Ruth, 74–75

Samaritans
history of, 117–18
and Jesus. *See* Jesus: encounters
with Samaritans
sojourner
assimilation, 105–6, 111–12
Christians as, 126–28
legislation. *See* Law: Old
Testament
terminology. *See* immigration:
terminology, biblical

virtues, 93, 109